D0782716

TAMBÚ

CURAÇAO'S AFRICAN-CARIBBEAN RITUAL
AND THE POLITICS OF MEMORY

NANETTE DE JONG

WITHDRAWN
UTSA Libraries

INDIANA UNIVERSITY PRESS
Bloomington and Indianapolis

This book is a publication of

Indiana University Press
601 North Morton Street
Bloomington, Indiana 47404-3797 USA

iupress.indiana.edu

Telephone orders 800-842-6796
Fax orders 812-855-7931

© 2012 by Nanette de Jong

All rights reserved
No part of this book may be reproduced or utilized in any form or
by any means, electronic or mechanical, including photocopying
and recording, or by any information storage and retrieval system,
without permission in writing from the publisher. The Association of
American University Presses' Resolution on Permissions constitutes
the only exception to this prohibition.

♾ The paper used in this publication meets the minimum
requirements of the American National Standard for Information
Sciences—Permanence of Paper for Printed Library Materials,
ANSI Z39.48-1992.

Manufactured in the United States of America

Library of Congress Cataloging-in-Publication Data

Jong, Nanette de, [date]
   Tambú : Curaçao's African-Caribbean ritual and the politics of
memory / Nanette de Jong.
      p. cm. — (Ethnomusicology multimedia)
   Includes bibliographical references and index.
   ISBN 978-0-253-35654-3 (cloth : alk. paper) — ISBN 978-0-253-
22337-1 (pbk. : alk. paper) — ISBN 978-0-253-00572-4 (electronic
book) 1. Tambú (Music)—Curaçao—History and criticism. 2. Blacks—
Curaçao—Music—History and cricism. 3. Music—Social aspects—
Curaçao. 4. Blacks—Curaçao—Rites and ceremonies. I. Title.
   ML3565.J67 2012
   781.62′96972986—dc23
                                                    2011035912

1 2 3 4 5   17 16 15 14 13 12

Library
University of Texas
at San Antonio

DEDICATED TO MY PARENTS,

Dr. Gerald and Mrs. Jeanette de Jong:

Batidó'i mi tobo,
Tokadó'i mi chapi

Player of my tambú,
Player of my chapi.

CONTENTS

Acknowledgments   *ix*

Introduction / Introducktorio:
Get Ready! / Poné Bo Kla!   1

PART 1. Habri: Here It Is, the History of Tambú!
Até Aki, Historia di Tambú!   13

1. The Story of Our Ancestors, the Story of Africa
E Kuenta di Nos Antepasados, e Kuenta di Afrika   15

2. Told through the Fierce Rhythms of the Drum
Kontá pa e Ritmonan Furioso di su Barí   30

3. The Laws Couldn't Keep Tambú Away.
The Church Couldn't Keep Tambú Away.
Leinan No Por a Tene Tambú Lew.
Misa No Por a Tene Tambú Lew.   49

PART 2. Será: Get Ready! Get Ready!
Poné Bo Kla! Poné Bo Kla!   71

4. Prepare for the Arrival of Our Ancestors
Prepará Bo pa e Jegada di Nos Antepasados   73

5. Clap Your Hands!
Bati Bo Mannan!   88

6. Come for the Party
Bin na e Fiesta   104

Conclusion/Conclui:
Are You Ready? Are You Ready to Hear the History of Tambú?
Bo Ta Kla? Bo Ta Kla pa Tende e Historia di Tambú?   117

Glossary of Terms Referring to Tambú   129

Bibliography   143

List of Interviews   151

Index   153

ACKNOWLEDGMENTS

I did not choose Curaçao as a research site as much as Curaçao chose me, or, perhaps, more aptly, Curaçao captured me, the unusual diversity of its music captivating my research interests, while the kindness and sincerity of the people enabled a rare sense of belonging. Although now a bit ironic, my initial plan for research was to explore the Petro pantheon of Haiti's Vodou religion. In preparation for this endeavor I attended separate language courses in French and Patois, I took university-led seminars in French Caribbean history, and I built up a library of essays and books on the topic. I excitedly made plans to relocate to Port-au-Prince, organizing contacts and finalizing a place of temporary residence. As the dates for my travel to Haiti drew closer, however, unrest between Haiti and the United States escalated. With the United States threatening a forced invasion, the prospective lenders of my research grant contracted their support, suggesting instead I reapply for research to another Caribbean country.

The eventual decision to focus on the Netherlands Antilles, surprisingly, did not come quickly or easily. Yet, once made, the decision revealed an overarching logic, and I remain surprised and even perplexed that the decision was so slow in coming. I am of Dutch American ancestry; my father (now deceased) was a major scholar of Dutch American history; and as a family we spent summers living in Den Haag. Moving my research to the Dutch Caribbean was not only reasonable; it felt "natural."

The "story," however, is not yet finished—Curaçao was not my first choice; Bonaire, a neighboring island was, with travel to Curaçao planned four to five months later. I bought my airline ticket, packed my suitcases, and prepared my departure. Arriving in Miami, however, I received news that the plane to Bonaire was canceled. Passengers were being rerouted to Curaçao, with flights to Bonaire scheduled one week later. Unexpectedly, I found myself comfortably settling into Curaçaoan life during that week: within the first few days of arrival I had met with—and even performed along-side—numerous local musicians, had found a suitable apartment, and had enrolled in an accelerated Papiamento language course. I never did travel to Bonaire during that initial trip; the unused airline voucher issued at the Miami International Airport remains tucked in my collected papers, serving as reminder that life's journeys cannot always be predicted.

My integration into Curaçaoan society definitely was eased by the fact that I am a musician. Well-versed in jazz and salsa performance, I served as a frequent guest flautist and regular member of several local groups and bands. Through the common ground of musical performance, I was thus able to connect with and gain the respect of Curaçaoan musicians and local audiences in ways that would otherwise have been impossible. Many of the conversations I engaged with local musicians occurred after gigs, when party hosts shut their doors to outside visitors, and offered drinks to the musicians and a few close friends. Without my flute-playing, these conversations would almost certainly have remained closed, and musicians likely would not have conversed so honestly and openly with me.

I have since traveled to Curaçao fourteen additional times, most trips planned around continuing the research for this book. It is with enormous gratitude that I thank the people of Curaçao for opening their lives to me, for embracing me as part of their family. They never shied away from my questions; they answered with grace, honesty, and candidness. Very special thanks go to the Salsbach and Arvelo families: Arnell, Michael, Claritza, Lalo, Diëllo, Viennaline (Ninki), Mafalda, Martijn "Shon Ma," Sherman, and, especially, Epifania "Fanny" Salsbach, who graciously opened her home and heart during my many visits and today stands as one of my dearest friends; and to the Wout family: Lucille, Jenny, Aura Rijke, Willem, and, particularly, John, for his unyielding generosity and friendship; and to Rose Mary Allen, Gilbert Bacilio, Errol "Toro" Colina, Boy Dap, Max Martina, the late Edgar Palm, and John James Willekes for their critical dialogues and observations. I have also been the beneficiary of exemplary generosity and support from Tambú followers and supporters, who shared their time and private lives despite overarching social, religious, and legal restrictions surrounding Tambú. Due to possible retribution, their names cannot be shared. My gratitude, therefore, cannot be fully served by these acknowledgments. Yet, my profound admiration and gratitude must be emphasized. It is inconceivable that this book would have taken its present form without their counsel and comments.

I have enjoyed a most cooperative relationship with colleagues at the International Centre for Music Studies at Newcastle University, and I am exceedingly grateful for their unwavering guidance and support. I also owe thanks to my friends at the Latino Center for Arts and Culture, the Paul Robeson Center, the Livingston College Honors Program, the Office of Diverse Community Affairs and LGBT, and the Office of Academic and Public Partnerships in the Arts and Humanities at Rutgers University for making possible many opportunities for work and play; particular thanks are offered to Isabel Nazario, Julio Nazario, Sandra Rocio Castro, Vilma Perez, and Glenda Daniel, whose years of encouragement, sometimes under difficult circumstances, have been essential to my finishing this manuscript.

The great Tambú singer and drum-maker Pincho gave diligently of his time, providing me with the benefit of his vast knowledge and expertise, for which I remain permanently in his debt. Lorna McDaniel has been a patient mentor and a constant resource. Rene Rosalia has served as an inspiration, rewarding me with his company and expertise. Jerry de Jong, Renee Baillargeon, Lester Monts, Stephanie Motz, Ian Biddle, and Richard Elliott provided great sources of insight and guidance. Additional thanks go to the South African "crew": George Suliali, Aqualine Suliali, Racquel Mair, and Yajaira Espinal Russell; and to the Congo "crew": Raison Newman Obalolayama and Ould Hamed Dicko Moulaye, for their boundless enthusiasm and support.

Finally, I thank the staff at the Centraal Historisch Archief in Curaçao and the Antilliana-Caribiana department of the Curaçao Public Library Foundation for indispensable assistance; and at Indiana University Press, I thank Dee Mortensen, for her support, understanding, and vision, and Louis Simon, for providing intelligent, meticulous, and consistent editing.

With the publication of this book marking the culmination of a life-changing fifteen years of my life, I have had the support of numerous mentors, colleagues, and friends—too many to mention. It would take a manuscript in itself to acknowledge by name everyone who assisted me in the various stages of this adventure. I will have to thank you all collectively for your endless support and patience. No one can know the full impact your lives have had on me.

To close, I am deeply grateful to my brother Owen for helping me from concept to completion; he pored over drafts of chapters and encouraged me to keep pushing forward. I also want to celebrate my parents, Gerald and Jeanette de Jong—it is impossible to imagine how this project would have been realized without their passion, inspiration, faith, and love. It is to them I dedicate this book.

Some portions of this work have been previously published as "The Tambú of Curaçao: Historical Projections and the Ritual Map of Experience," *Black Music Research Journal,* vol. 30.2 (Fall 2010), pp. 197–214. The author wishes to thank the University of Illinois Press for their kind permission. Some portions of this work have also been previously published as "Tambú: Commemorating the Past, Recasting the Present," *Transforming Anthropology,* vol. 16.1 (April 2008), pp. 32–41. The author wishes to thank the American Anthropological Association and Wiley-Blackwell Publishing for their kind permission. Appreciation is also extended to Ibrahim Lucas for making his photographs of Tambú dance available to me, and to Curaçao Historical Archives for providing photographs of Landhuis Santa Crus and of hotel performances of Tambú.

TAMBÚ

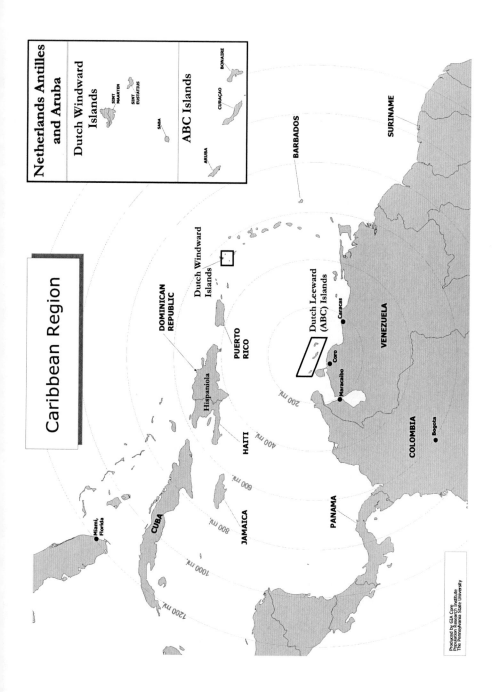

Caribbean Region

Netherlands Antilles and Aruba

Dutch Windward Islands

SINT MARTEN
SINT EUSTATIUS
SABA

ABC Islands

ARUBA
CURAÇAO
BONAIRE

BARBADOS

SURINAME

DOMINICAN REPUBLIC

Dutch Windward Islands

PUERTO RICO

Dutch Leeward (ABC) Islands

Caracas

VENEZUELA

Coro

Maracaibo

200 mi.

Hispaniola

HAITI

400 mi.

COLOMBIA

Bogota

600 mi.

JAMAICA

800 mi.

CUBA

1000 mi.

PANAMA

1200 mi.

Miami, Florida

Produced by GIA Core
Population Research Institute
The Pennsylvania State University

Poné Bo Kla![1]
(E Tambú di Pincho)

Poné bo kla! Poné bo kla!

Até aki, e historia di Tambú!
E kuenta di nos antepasados.
E kuenta di Afrika.
Até aki, e historia di Tambú!
Kontá pa e ritmonan furioso di su Tambú.
E texto di e Kantika por ta un pildora marga pa guli.
Pasobra Tambú no tin miedu di berdat.
Até aki, e historia di Tambú!
Wak ora nos ta balia!
Un pia na tera,
Planta firme manera e tronko di un palu.
Un pia ta liber,
Kla pa pusha, kla pa kore.
Até aki, e historia di Tambú!
Leinan no por a tene Tambú lew.
Misa no por a tene Tambú lew.
E ta aki. E ta nos. E ta nos historia.
E kuenta di nos antepasados.
E kuenta di Afrika.

Poné bo kla! Poné bo kla!
Prepará bo pa e jegada di nos antepasados.
Poné bo kla! Poné bo kla!
Partisipá na e baile.
Poné bo kla! Poné bo kla!
Bati bo mannan.
Poné bo kla! Poné bo kla!
Bin na e fiesta.

Bo ta kla?
Bo ta kla pa tende e historia di Tambú?

---

1. This Tambú was composed especially for the publication of this book, written by Sherwin "Pincho" Anita, one of Curaçao's most respected Tambú band leaders and singers.

Get Ready!
(A Tambú by Pincho)

Get ready! Get ready!

Here it is, the history of Tambú!
The story of our ancestors.
The story of Africa.
Here it is, the history of Tambú!
Told through the fierce rhythms of its drum.
The song text may be a bitter pill to swallow,
Because Tambú does not fear the truth.
Here it is, the history of Tambú!
Watch, as we dance!
One foot on the ground,
Planted, secure like the trunk of a tree.
One foot is free,
Ready to stomp, ready to run.
Here it is, the history of Tambú!
The laws couldn't keep Tambú away.
The church couldn't keep Tambú away.
It is here. It is us. It is our history.
The story of our ancestors.
The story of Africa.

Get ready! Get ready!
Prepare for the arrival of our ancestors.
Get ready! Get ready!
Join in the dance.
Get ready! Get ready!
Clap your hands.
Get ready! Get ready!
Come to the party.

Are you ready?
Are you ready to hear the history of Tambú?

Curaçao

Bandabou

Knip Bay

Caribbean Sea

San Juan Bay

Bullen Bay

St. Joris Bay

Willemstad

Bandariba

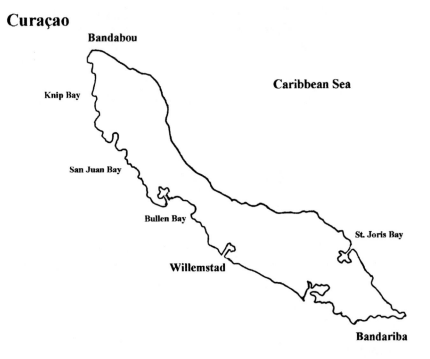

Introduction: Get Ready!
Introduktorio: Poné Bo Kla!

Whether it is celebrated or rejected, attended to or ignored, the past is omnipresent. —DAVID LOWENTHAL

From the air, Curaçao looks narrow and flat. It appears stark and quiet, its dry desert plains scattered with clusters of tall cacti, its shores noticeably rocky, dotted with divi-divi trees and Dutch-styled windmills. Stepping off my plane means leaving my air-conditioned reverie to enter the warm humid air that breathes the sudden realization: this is my home for the next year. I am here to study Curaçaoan culture—to scout the island for its music and the country's African-based ritual rhythms.

I slide into the back seat of a taxi. With one glance at my hotel address, the taxi driver is off, his pace brisk, braking only occasionally for the potholes and speed bumps. We are on our way to the central city of Willemstad, the capital of Curaçao. Unlike many other islands, Curaçao has not gained colonial independence. Instead, after World War II it acquired a measure of autonomy as a member of the Netherlands Antilles; and, with the dissolution of the Netherlands Antilles in October 2010, Curaçao became a constituent country within the Kingdom of the Netherlands, to which it remains economically, politically, and socially tied.[2]

2. The Netherlands Antilles had comprised Aruba, Bonaire, and Curaçao (known as the Windward Antilles, due to their location in the eastern end of the Caribbean Sea) and Saba, Sint Eustatius, and Sint Maarten (defined collectively as the Leeward Antilles, due to their northern location). Aruba became an independent entity in 1986 (the crusade toward gaining full independence was halted in 1990, due to internal strife among Aruban citizens). With the recent (October 2010) dissolution of the Netherlands Antilles, the islands of Bonaire, Sint Eustatius, and Saba have become "public bodies" of the Kingdom of the Netherlands, which, collectively known as Caribbean Netherlands or BES islands, are considered overseas territories of the European Union; while the islands of Curaçao and Sint Maarten have become constituent countries within the Kingdom of the Netherlands.

Curaçao is the largest island of the Dutch Caribbean (171 square miles), and, with a population over 140,000, houses nearly two-thirds of the entire Dutch Caribbean population. Located thirty-five miles north of Venezuela and forty-two miles east of Aruba, Curaçao provides the perfect location for the tourist: it is outside the hurricane belt, with an average year-round temperature of 80 degrees. The city of Willemstad is divided by a port channel, Sint Annabaai ("Saint Anna Bay"), enclosed by rugged hills. One side of the harbor, called Punda ("The Point"), is a popular shopping stop for tourists—its picturesque colonial-styled buildings are topped with red-gabled, tiled roofs, and are painted in a kaleidoscope of colors, including pink, blue, green, and purple. Reminiscent of Amsterdam, Rotterdam, and the other Dutch cities, Curaçao's architectural landscape provides a strange familiarity to the many Dutch tourists who head for Curaçao for their vacations each year. The other side of Willemstad, called Otrobanda ("The Other Side"), attracts the local shoppers—"it has the best deals in town," one Curaçaoan woman later shared with me. Its maze of winding streets are flanked by rows of small, colonial houses. Although these roads appear too narrow to pass by car, they sustain heavy traffic, morning, noon, and night.

Otrobanda and Punda are connected by two different bridges, Queen Emma and Queen Juliana, both named after popular Dutch royalty. Queen Emma is a wooden-planked floating bridge, ready to open and fold against the Otrobanda shore when ships enter or exit the harbor. When the bridge is open, pedestrians are forced to board ferries which shuttle them back and forth across the channel. While automobiles were once permitted to cross the Queen Emma Bridge, they are now restricted to Queen Juliana, a four-lane, 200-foot-high structure built in 1975. "The Queen Juliana Bridge is the tallest bridge in the Caribbean," my taxi driver proudly states as he repeatedly changes gears, the taxi slowly edging its way to the top. The view from Queen Juliana is magnificent. Looking out toward the sea, both Punda and Otrobanda are visible as one collective city. The opposite direction provides bird's-eye views of the many oil refineries set along the inner harbor coast. "Among the largest refinery businesses in the world," the taxi driver says, again with pride.

My hotel is a tiny building tucked between the shops of Otrobanda. Quickly checking into my room means I am free to explore the streets of my new island neighborhood. Within moments of the walk, it becomes apparent that Curaçao embraces a distinct cultural diversity. The street vendors and cafes tout the Dutch favorites *frikandel* (sausages) and *vlees bitterballen* (beef meatballs), as well as dishes from Indonesia—*nasi goreng* and *bami goreng;* Surinam—*bruine bonen* (brown beans) and *pinda soep* (peanut soup); Portugal—*bakiou* (salted codfish, known as bacalhão in Portugal); and India—*samosa* (potato stuffed pastry) and *chana* (spicy chickpeas); not to mention the many popular Curaçaoan sweets—*pan seiku* (peanuts in brown sugar) and *kokada* (freshly shaved coconut in white sugar). Conversations among passersby breathe the island's unusual mix of languages. While Dutch may be considered the "official" language of Curaçao, *Papiamento* (an indigenous creole blend of Portuguese, Dutch, Spanish, and a myriad of West African languages) is also popularly spoken, as are Spanish and English. The different languages are exchanged easily in conversation, with two or more spoken within a single discussion.

The same diversity shows itself in the music. Contemporary *salsa*, Surinamese *kaseko*, Mexican *mariachi*, and Colombian *cumbia* are piped loudly into downtown stores and restaurants. Yet, as I eventually learn, the Antillean waltz, a creole variation on the European dance, dominates the restaurants and bars in rural outskirts. Played on the *ka'i orgel* (mechanical barrel organ) and accompanied by the *wiri* (an indigenous instrument consisting of a long piece of serrated metal over which a thin metal stick is scraped), the Antillean waltz garners large crowds, with local audiences cramming onto the dance floor, eager to take part (De Jong 2003a). Visit a private, local party, called *Comback,* and you will hear traditional Cuban music from the 1920s, performed by a live band or played from original 78-rpm recordings (De Jong 2003b). Noticeably missing from this diverse musical landscape, however, are Curaçao's indigenous African rhythms. Performances of Tambú—perhaps the island's most African-inspired form—are extremely difficult to find. Only after considerable investigation does one realize that the secular Tambú is ascribed a specific season (November to January), and that the religious Tambú is shrouded in secrecy.

With roots dating back to the slavery period, Tambú emerged as a vehicle through which modern Curaçaoans of African descent could maintain cultural links with the African continent. Rhythm and dance transported Tambú participants back through time, along the African coasts and within the mainland territories, affording Afro-Curaçaoans the opportunity to translate an invisible past into a tangible present. Tambú conflated the Afro-Curaçaoan desire for an autonomous cultural identity with the reality of Curaçao's long history of slavery and colonialism. The religion to which Tambú served as accompaniment was called *Montamentu* during the years of slavery. Montamentu purposely equated specific African deities with corresponding Catholic saints, while simultaneously paying homage to African and Amerindian ancestral spirits. In this way, the imbalance between a formerly enslaved people and their proprietors blurred as a cultural synthesis emerged. Participants embraced (or rejected) perceived memories from a veritable smorgasbord of possibilities; and by selective picking and choosing, descendants of Afro-Curaçaoan former slaves extended the concept of corporeal emancipation to social identity, enabling an African-centered historical consciousness to take root in a New World context.

To borrow from Michel-Rolph Trouillot, Tambú was "born against all odds" (Trouillot 2002: 191). It "emerged against the expectations and wishes of plantation owners and their European patrons" (ibid.), resonating with African myths and histories that refused to disappear with the Middle Passage. Tambú's emergence represents a tenuous and provisional process of cultural negotiation known as creolization. From a polyglot origin and a plethora of cultural influences, it emerged almost miraculously, transforming "heterogeneous crowds"—as Sidney Mintz and Richard Price have defined the first African peoples arriving in the New World (1992: 10)—into individual, autonomous creole cultures. As a product of the creolization process, Tambú changed and developed according to the particular colonial government and plantation politics experienced by the Africans on Curaçao.

In recent years, the Tambú has undergone multiple transformations that in the end have not only transcended but eclipsed the ritual's African-centered archetype. It stepped up to fill a diversity of social roles and purposes, both sacred and secular, its form and meaning evolving in accordance with the immediate needs and interests of Curaçao's evolving African community. As a sacred ritual, it continued to facilitate the worship of deities and communion with ancestors; as a secular practice, it became tantamount to an oral newspaper—a medium for the documentation of local news and gossip, and for its dissemination to the island's distant corners. In its more recent evolution, it has produced a renowned Curaçaoan New Year's event through which bad luck perceived to have accrued during the previous year may ostensibly be driven away. In yet another, newer transformation, this event, during the so-called Tambú Season, has become an occasion in which Curaçaoan youth revel in what they now consider party music.

A major factor guiding these transformations has been a consensual process of forgetting among the Afro-Curaçaoan people themselves. Tambú faced chronic legal and religious disapproval during slavery, which drove the ritual underground. Because the church and state have continued their denouncement of Tambú, the ritual—even in its secular forms—enjoys only a limited general acceptance and appreciation even today. In fact, few Curaçaoans even recognize the term *Montamentu*. Instead, most have adopted the disparaging term introduced by Catholic priests and Dutch slavers centuries earlier—*Brua* ("witch"), or have come to apply to the religious ritual the general term *Tambú*. Because Tambú performances have been restricted to the months of November, December, and January, many Curaçaoans have also come to think of Tambú as Christmas music. As a result, some Curaçaoans today, particularly among the younger generation, are unaware of Tambú's traditional African past.

Our sense of history often plays tricks on us—human memory lacks the cold precision of a computer hard drive. To paraphrase one of the catchphrases of computer parlance: Info in; info out. Human memory is not that simple. It seldom "sees" exactly, nor does it retain much in exact form. The human tendency is to adjust and change details to suit immediate or long-term perceived personal and social needs. This treasury "of innumerable images of all kinds," as St. Anthony once reflected on human memory, ultimately serves to define us individually and in groups.

Memory and its loss transcend experience strategically, and give rise to interpretation. Edward Bruner, who defines experience as "how events are received by consciousness" (1986: 4), distinguishes it from expression, or "how individual experience is formed and articulated" (ibid.: 5). Stories emerge from the recounting of experience, providing a basis on which certain life lessons become articulated through selective accounts of the actual past. Perception and definition of self, therefore, are guided by recalled information colored by subsequent interpretation, as fluid as the social or personal dynamics of their source. "The things of the past are never viewed in their true perspective," writes Friedrich Nietzsche, asserting that "value and perspective change with the individual [or nation] . . . looking back" (1957: 19). From this perspective, the purpose of memory is not to store information, but to provide a forum via which to make sense of that information. With memory and its loss existing as two sides of the same coin, each presupposing the other's existence, it is the selectivity of what is forgotten that helps define the importance of what is remembered. As a consequence, it becomes fruitless to discuss whether or not a particular event corresponds to the actual past: what become paramount are the specific conditions under which such a memory is constructed, as well as the personal and social implications of memories held.

What does it mean for a cultural community to remember? Memory forms the fabric of human life, affecting everything from the ability to perform simple, everyday tasks to the recognition of the self. Memory establishes life's continuity; memory gives meaning to the present, as each moment is constituted by the past. As the means by which we remember who we are, memory provides the very core of identity. Yet the process of cultural memory is bound up in complex political stakes and meanings. To define a memory as culture is, in effect, to enter into a debate about what that memory means. This process does not efface the individual but rather involves the interaction of individuals in the creation of cultural meaning.

Every social group defines itself by its processing and construction of memories of its past. While one remembers within and as part of a social group, it is the meshing of a group's individual remembrances that creates a collective memory. It is, Eric Halbwachs writes, a complex process of exchange and negotiation with "individual[s] remember[ing] by placing [themselves] in the perspective of the group" (1980: 40).

When the state becomes involved in the memory-making process, a collective memory becomes political, and it is fair to ask just who is "collecting" the early experiences and ultimately shaping them into "collective memories." James Young, in an effort to demonstrate that memory does not necessarily represent actual understanding regarding the past, introduces the term "collected memory." Young writes that "The society's memory might be regarded as an aggregate collection of its members' many, often competing memories. If societies remember, it is only insofar as their institutions and rituals organize, shape, even inspire their constituents' memories. For a society's memory cannot exist outside of those people who do the remembering—even if such memory happens to be at the society's bidding, in its name" (1993: xi). A point of departure for the holistic study of any given community, then, will be its perceived memories—some are so tinted that recollection is cast in a golden hue, interpreted through a romanticizing filter; others, through guilt or distorting emotion, are cast in darker shades.

The scrutiny paid to history, therefore, must be extended to include those rituals that commemorate history. Like memory and history, they too may alter in meaning and context. Commemorative rituals enable the past to be recast within frameworks that facilitate cultural coherence and unity, and as such, can be used to justify just about any plan people may have in mind—be it benevolent or malevolent. They may be linked to societal leaders, manipulated for purposes of legitimizing artificially constructed pasts; or they can be adopted to mythologize the past, used by communities to reappraise or even embellish history. Tambú is one of the dominant routes via which Africa comes to the minds of Curaçaoans. A central concern posed in this book is defining what happens when it ceases to be a vehicle for remembering Africa or is linked to memories other than Africa.

Initially, my research goal was to use Tambú to uncover an African past reinvented on Curaçao. What emerged more clearly, however, were not Tambú's implied links to history, but rather the many varied interpretations of and reactions to those links by the Curaçaoan people. For example, followers of the Catholic Church on Curaçao generally view the ritual as sinful and vulgar, with priests using their pulpits to provide weekly diatribes against Tambú's "evil character." Members of the Dutch government, on the other hand, view Tambú as a deterrent to establishing social order on Curaçao, and continue to institute laws meant to limit participation. Many Afro-Curaçaoans, having found involvement risky, made the difficult decision to abandon their association with Tambú. With Afro-Curaçaoans now rejecting the ritual for reasons promoted by church and state—"Tambú is evil"; "Tambú is low class"; "Decent women do not participate in Tambú"— Tambú, through manipulation, has come full circle. These complexities and conflicts emerge as products of pluralism; they reveal the ways Curaçao's distinct cultural groups maintain very different values and ways of looking at life. Such cultural pluralism played a fundamental role in stimulating, defining, and filtering African memories on Curaçao, and assumes definition and disjuncture only when examined within the context of the island's larger historical narrative.

The Spaniards were the first Europeans to claim Curaçao (in 1492). What they discovered was an island very different than what they had expected. Its shortcomings of climate and poor soil condition earned Curaçao the epithet *isla inútil* ("useless island"). When gold was discovered among the nearby Spanish colonies of Venezuela and Colombia, Curaçao went largely ignored, becoming instead dominated by *Indieros*—those who hunted and captured native Arawaks for the purpose of slavery. Then in 1634, the Dutch took possession (Goslinga 1971: 264)[3] of the island. The

Dutch-owned *West Indische Compaigne* (translated in English as West Indies Company, commonly referred to by its acronym, WIC) took advantage of the island's natural harbors to broaden its participation in the New World slave trade, transforming the island into a primary detention facility and point of departure for approximately half a million Africans sold into slavery elsewhere in the New World (Postma 1975: 237). *Negotie slaven* ("slaves for trade") was the term used to denote the large numbers of Africans sold throughout the Caribbean and South America. Those marked unsaleable (largely due to illness or old age) remained on Curaçao, and were called *manquerons* ("unsaleable ones").

When the savvy Dutch businessmen realized that other European colonialists were highly interested in purchasing slaves already indoctrinated into Christianity, they seized the opportunity of adding monetary value to their human commodity: the WIC obliged paying customers by imposing religious training on all negotie slaven. Uninterested in converting the Africans themselves, the Dutch commissioned priests from nearby Venezuela (Curaçao and Venezuela are just forty miles apart) to travel to the island to indoctrinate negotie slaven by means of regular mass services and religious education.

By eighteenth-century standards, Curaçao was regarded as a haven of religious tolerance, although this had occurred largely as an unplanned by-product of capitalism and profit. Curaçao's widespread reputation attracted persecuted religious groups from around the world. The largest incoming religious group was comprised of Sephardic Jews from New Holland (an area of northeastern Brazil, including Recife and Pernambuco, that was ruled by the Dutch during the seventeenth century). So large was this influx that between 1725 and 1770, Sephardics actually outnumbered Curaçao's Dutch, although Curaçao's Sephardic element became a separate social enclave.

Afro-Curaçaoans gained their physical freedom when slavery was abolished in 1863. Because slavery had been Curaçao's foremost industry, its abolishment caused considerable economic adversity. Most white Hollanders returned to the Netherlands; those who remained retained positions of governmental authority and social prominence; and Afro-Curaçaoans were

---

3. At the time of the Dutch conquest, the island's population consisted of thirty-two Spaniards and about five hundred Arawaks, whom the Dutch quickly transported (at their own expense) to Venezuela, leaving only seventy-five Arawaks on the island (Goslinga 1971: 267–269).

forced to travel outside the island for work. Cuba became the most popular destination, with Afro-Curaçaoans joining Chinese, Mexican, Haitian, and Jamaican nationals who also sought employment in Cuba's lucrative sugar industry. Along with the existing Afro-Cuban population from the island's own slave days under Spain, these groups comprised the large workforce. While the pay was poor, jobs were available, and the Cuban sugar industry remained the employment destination of choice for Afro-Curaçaoans well into the early years of the twentieth century (Paula 1978: 22–25). It is estimated that during the 1920s and '30s, over half the male Afro-Curaçaoan workforce migrated to Cuba (Allen 1989).[4]

By the late 1930s, prospects for employment on Curaçao suddenly improved with an unparalleled economic boom responding to the giant Dutch oil corporation Shell's burgeoning interest in South American oil. The establishment of new refineries created a corresponding need for workers at all skill levels (Paula 1978). To meet these new employment demands, the Curaçaoan government, which had largely ignored reports of mistreatment on Cuba, began making arrangements during the 1930s for the repatriation of its emigrant workforce and began offering incentives for them to return (Soest 1977: 125; Römer 1977: 113–114).[5] Although many elected to remain on Cuba to build their own Antillean community there, scores of Afro-Curaçaoans, many now with strong family connections to Cuba, began to stream back to their home island (Paula 1978: 59–61).

As Shell continued to expand, it became necessary for the company to advertise for skilled and unskilled workers outside Curaçao, including Venezuela, the British West Indies, the Dominican Republic, Surinam (Dutch Guiana), Lebanon, Syria, and Romania (the majority of whom were Ashkenazi Jews fleeing persecution in the years leading up to the Second World War) (Gomes Casseres 1984: 24). Within decades, the number of immigrants living on Curaçao exceeded some fifty thousand, with the government recording over forty nationalities in its registrar, and Curaçao fast becoming

---

4. The great numbers were due in part to the emergence of certain employment agreements, known as *braceros Antillanos negros*. These agreements were designed to undercut the local Afro-Cuban workers and their demands for more reasonable wages. Drawn up by the sugar industry itself, these employment agreements authorized the importation of increasing numbers of black Caribbean manual laborers willing to work on the plantations for low wages (Pérez 1995).

5. Although the number of migrants traveling to Cuba declined after the government's plea, it was not until 1948 that it finally ceased completely (Paula 1978: 59–61).

one of the most ethnically and culturally diverse islands in the Caribbean (Rupert 2002).

Research on Tambú has tended to follow lines traced by historians of Curacao's colonial past, with scholars broadly indicating the ritual's colonial beginnings (e.g., Goslinga 1956, 1971, 1977, 1985, 1990, 1993; Hartog 1956–1964, 1961; Postma 1990a, 1990b, 2003). The earliest writings come from Curaçao's self-proclaimed folklorists Elis Juliana, a writer and visual artist (1976, 1983, 1987, 1990), and the priest Paul Brenneker (1961, 1971, 1974, 1975), whose papers and short books gave initial insights into Tambú's slave origins and traditional roles. The most in-depth study on Tambú to date, a dissertation by the anthropologist Rene Rosalia, describes the early Tambú types, and lists the laws developed by the Dutch government to limit Tambú participation (1997). Whereas Rosalia raises interesting questions about the climate of opposition against Tambú, this book will link adverse political policy to the ongoing development of the genre, and to the flows of society, thus highlighting Tambú's potential insights into how our sense of tradition can have ideological consequences by helping to define a culture and subculture.

This book introduces Tambú as a mode for examining Afro-Curaçaoan society by showing how the ritual has moved both within and against the contexts of history and memory. Tambú stands at the busy intersection of "a culture in motion" (Rosaldo 1988), its various types each affected by, and indeed part of, society. Tambú survives in the balance of memory and history, existing in a "process of continually beginning, continually ending" (Carter 1987: xxiv), miraculously and powerfully transforming history into memory, imbuing memory with history. Examining how Afro-Curaçaoans' relationship with Tambú has framed the manner by which they remember the past exposes the tenuous nature of history. It shows how history can be produced, reinvented, circulated, and consumed, with ritual itself becoming a relative category for representing that process.

It is not difficult to establish reasons why colonialism has plagued the collective memory of slave communities—colonizers leave indelible imprints on the collective psyche of the colonized. However, for the Curaçaoans, who remain politically and economically tied to the Kingdom of the Netherlands, that imposing process has continued into the twenty-first century. Examining Tambú in light of this continued process of colonization exposes some of the complexities involved in "collected memory." To what extent does a colonized society affect how a colonized people ultimately see the world? What is memory's relation to people's identification with the nation as a whole? Why is memory so often adopted as a tool of colonization by oppressors? What does cultural forgetting show about the possibilities and limits of history? These questions acknowledge the influence political values have on notions of time and history. By answering them, Tambú is exposed as both a cultural event and a political phenomenon. As revealed in this book, politics has everything to do with Tambú, creating conflicts and complexities, generating ambiguities and dualisms that have ultimately shaped—and continue to reshape—the Afro-Curaçaoan ethos.

The organization of this book is meant to mirror Tambú's forms. Very briefly, the form of Tambú can be described as having two main parts, preceded by a short introduction. Each section has its own purpose and role: the introduction communicates the song's title or basic theme; the first main section provides the central storyline, with audiences expected to stand in quiet reflection; and the second main section emphasizes participation, with bystanders free to respond in dance and song. The Tambú concludes with the solo singer providing one last statement; the audience one last response.

In imitation, this book, too, is divided into two main parts, preceded by an introduction, ending with a final call and response. Much like the introduction to Tambú, this introduction presents the book's topic. It confronts the challenges involved in memory studies, and explains how Tambú can be viewed as a vehicle for negotiating notions of history and remembering. Part 1, emulating the first main section in Tambú, encourages an understanding of and appreciation for the book's topic. Its chapters provide the basic background information on Tambú, including an investigation into its creole origins; a description of Tambú's musical structure, instrumentation, and dance practices; a review of the different Tambú types; and a critique of the role the church and state have had in the development of Tambú and the current, contradictory interpretations of history. After the reader has become versed in the mechanisms of Tambú, including its musical structure and social history, part 2 is introduced. Like the second section of its musical counterpart, part 2 is focused on audience participation. Each chapter presents different audience responses to Tambú, uncovering the varied opportunities for participation, demonstrating how a people's approach to Tambú ultimately defines their relationship to both past and present. The writing in part 2 shifts its focus to the voice of the first person. Its inclusion of personal accounts, including that of the author, is intended to pull readers more deeply into the participatory nature of Tambú, telling the story in real time as a way to bring the reader closer to the role of participant. The text to the Tambú song by Pincho, titled *"Poné Bo Kla!"* ("Get Ready!"), is used in this book to mark its sections, with individual verses providing headings and subheadings.

◊◊◊◊◊

"Poné Bo Kla!" The Tambú leader is calling. "Get Ready!" he sings his announcement in preparation for the Tambú event. This is our signal. Quickly, yet quietly, we gather around the lead singer, sitting in preparation to hear the story he will tell. *"Até aki, e historia di Tambú!"* "Here it is, the history of Tambú!" the singer begins. Part 1 is about to commence.

PART 1.

Habrí: Here It Is, the History of Tambú!
Até Aki, Historia di Tambú!

The Story of Our Ancestors, the Story of Africa
E Kuenta di Nos Antepasados, e Kuenta di Afrika

It is a process which involves the creation of entirely new culture
patterns out of the fragmented pieces of historically separate systems.
—JAY EDWARDS

Creolization, the evolutionary development of Afro-Caribbean culture, began when conditions allowed distinct cultural memories to regain meaningfulness within a New World context. Through a process of negotiation, certain histories continued; others became inverted or disappeared altogether.
In the end, creolization enabled diverse African cultures to mediate their differences within a new collective construct, legitimizing their cultural presence in the New World. Between layers of antecedents, the creole form exists
at the intersection of numerous cultural processes: between social and individual experience, between cultural Selves and Others, between retained and
discarded histories and identities, and between colonizers and colonized.

Diverse African nationals entered into a process of creolization, emerging finally as "hybrid societies . . . mosaics of borderlands where cultures
jostled and converged in combinations and permutations of dizzying com-

plexity" (Morgan 1997: 142). The history of creolization, then, traces the development of an alloy-culture from which much has been burned away. The mechanism for this process was set in motion quite inadvertently by white Europeans, whose ambitious economic vision for the New World squeezed maximum profitability out of minimum investment through unpaid slave labor. Toward this end, Africans of many cultural backgrounds, social statuses, and spiritual beliefs were captured and chained, transported within the holds of ships and forcibly relocated to the Caribbean, where they labored on the plantations or were resold elsewhere in the Americas.

According to Sidney Mintz and Richard Price, the multiplicity of African cultures "reach[ing] the New World did not compose, at [that] moment, groups" (1992: 10). Rather, the experience of slavery united the Africans, however diverse their backgrounds and cultures, compelling them to conform to the standards and expectations of the dominant white society. Although slavery eventually ended, emancipation failed to bring assimilation into the dominant culture, which was still unwilling to embrace blacks as equals. Emancipation, when it came, merely had the effect of cooling the New World "melting pot," and new cultural identities began to congeal. In the end, creolization enabled diverse African peoples to mediate differences within a new collective construct, and to redefine a cultural presence in the New World (Khan 2004: 4).

Montamentu, the religion for which Tambú served as accompaniment, decrees a modern cultural foothold based on abstract perceived Africanness, a hybrid adaptation of remembered African origins marked by their adaptation to the New World experience. Its emergence indicated the formation of a common identity and collective memory among the Afro-Curaçaoan people. To study Montamentu, then, is to examine one of the earliest examples of Afro-Curaçaoan collective memory. Its study reveals a dendrochronology—a history articulated in layered chapters. Just as cross sections of an ancient tree reveal secrets of climatology and other life circumstances to those able to interpret what they see, so too does the cultural stratum of Montamentu reveal to ethnologists the changing historical contexts of its growth and survival. Because creolization is bound to political and social stakes and meanings, unraveling its threads within Montamentu uncovers hidden complexities distinct to Curaçao's unique cultural encounters. Today's historians confront in Montamentu (and creolization in general) that which Trouillot calls the "ultimate challenge [of uncovering cultural] roots" (1995: xix).

Of the total 500,000 or so Africans who passed through Curaçao during the slave years, only some 2,300 were to remain permanently on the island. As previously stated, this created on Curacao two distinct slave communities: the *negotie slaven*, which was in a constant state of flux; and the other, the *manquerons*, which, much smaller in number, was static. The continuing turnover and growing diversity of the negotie slaven brought fresh supplies of African traditions to the island. Manquerons, forced to remain on Curaçao, were generally pressed into service as common laborers (Postma 1975: 237; Goslinga 1971: 362). As may be surmised, they came to connect with the dominant Dutch on an ongoing personal basis. Servants gained closest access to Dutch culture, often quartered within the *landhuis* ("plantation house") located on the grounds of estates they served, but every level of interaction and cultural exchange took place (Hartog 1961: 173). On the other hand, outside of marketing negotie slaven to other island plantations, Curaçaoan slavers maintained very little close contact with the negotie slaven. They were imprisoned as they were within the confines of Curaçao's two large detention camps—both located far from the homes of the Dutch; and, during their stay on Curaçao, their care fell to the island's lowest manqueron servants. Neither black subgroup represented to the Dutch a separate entity (Postma 1975: 271). The exchange of ideas between the negotie slaven and the manquerons produced a number of cultural by-products, including the Afro-syncretized religion, Montamentu. Because Dutch interests were largely focused on trade and profits, the goal of Christian proselytizing (which motivated other European colonialists) was not a high priority, and Montamentu, when it did evolve, was met with little interference from the island's dominant culture.

Africans taken into slavery through the Dutch *West Indische Compaigne* came predominantly from two geographical regions: the Angolan coast (roughly the area between Cameroon and the Congo River) and the region of West Africa. While the cultural foundation of Montamentu may be traced to these two African regions, sleuthing out the specific Old World antecedents presents a Gordian knot unlikely to be fully disentangled. Records, where they exist, tend to offer inconclusive evidence of slave origins, and often concentrate (nearly exclusively) on the Africans captured in the western coastal regions. While it is likely much will never be fully understood, modern research continues to pursue the challenge. Employing nontraditional means of deciphering the evidence becomes not just a possible option, but a real necessity.

The examination of ship logs kept by Dutch slavers yields cargo descriptions and lists from which theories of possible African derivations can be construed. It should be borne in mind, however, that such cargo descriptions were recorded not so much to document the nationalities and cultural backgrounds of African people as they were to inscribe inventory of trade. Lorna McDaniel shows that one practical reason for recording the national backgrounds of slave cargoes in the logs of ships was to better manage prisoners during the Middle Passage. Since certain African nations were involved in ongoing wars with other nations, separating these battling culture groups during the long journey was essential (McDaniel 1998: 36).

Because the ship logs emerged for reasons of trade, no standard classification system was developed, or even encouraged. As a result, misspellings and spelling modifications frequently occurred in the logs. Decoding these flaws represents a constant challenge to anyone attempting to use them as historical references. Often the African port of exit was used as a nation name. As occurred, Africans were captured in one area of Africa and then sold in another. These Africans usually were logged into the ship documents by the name of the African port of exit, rather than their actual nation of origin. *Cape Lahou* (also written as Cape LaHou) is one such example. Located on the mouth of the Ivory Coast, Cape Lahou became a terminology used for nation distinction (Curtin 1969: 185–186). Similarly, the trading station of *Kromatine* (also spelled *Cromanti, Kormantine,* and *Cormantine*) in Ghana was employed for identification purposes. Frequently, the language of a culture group became used as national title. *Mallais* (also written as *Malais* and *Malé*) was the language spoken by the Ewe-Fon people of Dahomey, yet during slavery *Mallais* evolved into a title used by slave captains to distinguish nationality (Wooding 1981: 21–23). Furthermore, ship's logs were rarely adjusted to reflect the innumerable prisoners who, having perished at sea, were unceremoniously tossed overboard (Curtin 1969; McDaniel 1998; Goslinga 1971). Although slave ship logs are a good starting point in the search for African origins in the Americas, they remain problematic, demanding constant review.

It must also be noted that slaves of certain African nationalities were perceived to be superior to others, and therefore might be expected to command top prices in the marketplace. Adding particularly to the confusion today is the fact that unprincipled proprietors are known to have deliberately misassigned national origins in order to capitalize on the higher prices. Dutch historian Jan Jacob Hartsinck speaks to this phenomenon in *Be-*

schrijving van Guiana of de Wilde Kust, in Zuid-Amerika (1770). Hartsinck gives this example of how some Dutch notoriously misrepresented the national background of incoming Africans: "The best slaves in the land [according to popular preference] have scratches on their foreheads" (referring to culture-specific decorative scarring). Hartsinck reports that some slavers were not above inflicting similar physical markings upon African slaves of other nationalities, hoping to fool purchasers into paying higher prices for their slaves. In the words of Hartsinck:

> We hope that our readers will not be displeased, especially those who are interested, if we give some descriptions of various kinds concerning the nature and marks [tokens, signs] of these people that distinguish them from each other; but one must be careful, however, because black slave-dealers may change these marks to their advantage and in that manner [transform] the poorer kind of Negroes [into something better than what they really are].
> (Hartsinck 1770: 918)

European participation in the African slave trade began with the Portuguese, whose interest expanded geometrically when it colonized immense Brazil, literally encompassing half a continent (Alden 1973; Boxer 1969). African slave labor comprised virtually the entirety of the Brazilian plantation workforce, making Brazil the leading importer of African slaves in the New World (Rawley 1981: 40–41). The bulk of the slave workforce came from Angola, and Philip Curtin estimates Angolans represented over 70 percent of Brazil's entire slave population (Curtin 1969). When Portugal found itself drawn into internal conflicts with Spain, its overseas territory became a secondary concern—and easy prey for outside takeovers. The Netherlands (known during the slave years as the United Provinces or Dutch Republic) was the major beneficiary of the weakened empire. The largest Dutch acquisition, comprising most of northeastern Brazil, was rechristened *New Holland,* and became the first Dutch plantation colony. Administration of the Dutch Republic's New World possessions was left to the *West Indische Compaigne,* chartered in 1621 (Boxer 1957: 27; Emmer 1981: 71–72; Postma 1990a: 15).

The WIC soon realized that New Holland's sugar-based plantation economy stood in need of an increasingly large workforce. "It is not possible to accomplish anything in Brazil without slaves," were the words of New Holland's first acting governor (Boxer 1957: 83). Unable to entice enough mainland Dutch to relocate to New Holland, the WIC had little choice but to persuade farmers who served under Portuguese rule to remain. Those farmers who agreed to stay during the Dutch occupation made the provisional request that an Angolan slave workforce be maintained—they were already accustomed to working with Angolan laborers, and had no interest in dealing with any other African culture group. In an effort to meet the demands, the WIC fought to expand its African holdings to include Angola. Within a few short decades, the Dutch Republic successfully drove the Portuguese from the African coastal trading stations of Luanda and Benguela, as well as the islands of São Thomé and Annabon, before eventually capturing Portugal's last remaining coastal station of Axim. Under Dutch rule, the exportation of Angolan slaves was stepped up. The WIC, which had virtually ignored Curaçao prior to its acquisition of New Holland, now looked to transform the island into a slave detention facility, where Africans could be brought before being shipped elsewhere. An estimated fifteen thousand Angolans passed through Luanda alone during Dutch occupation, with most channeled through Curaçao before heading to New Holland (Barlaeus 1647: 206–207; Boxer 1957: 106–108; Postma 1975: 26). The Angolan influence, therefore, manifested itself early on Curaçao, and has remained there—as evidenced by the presence of several cultural indicators.

The origin of Tambú has become associated with the arrival of the Angolans, primarily through the research of historian Luis Arturo Dominguez, who has traced Tambú's roots to a larger Angolan tradition of stick fighting (1988). As he explained it, Tambú derived from an acrobatic sparring ritual used during times of war in Angola. Part of a collection of *sanga* (or "war dances"), Tambú tested and rehearsed the skills of hand-to-hand combat and stick weaponry (Tavares 1984). It signified "an instrument of organization of the physical, individual, and community defense (weapon)" (Thornton 1988: 362), with "the ability to twist, leap, and dodge to avoid arrows or the blows of opponents" considered central (ibid.).

Stick fighting assumed different styles in the Caribbean, with participants' ethnic backgrounds and training guiding the individual transformations. In Trinidad, the stick fight *kalenda* (sometimes referred to as *bamboula*) emerged, testing agility and dexterity to the accompaniment of drums and chants (Liverpool 2001). In Bahia, Brazil, the stick dance *maculelê* surfaced, with the *grimas* (fighting sticks) serving also as musical instruments, providing the rhythmic accompaniment to wielders' acrobatic moves. The Curaçaoan version is called *kokomakaku*, its name taken from the island shrub *coco maque*, from whose trunks the combat fighting sticks were traditionally constructed (Brenneker 1975). Kokomakaku was a "game of skills," explains Brenneker and Juliana (Brenneker 1975, 1971; Juliana 1983, 1990). Two contestants sparred within a ring of spectators, sticks in hand, dancing and jumping to the rhythms of a single drum, known as *tambú*. The drummer would play a standard rhythmic pattern (transcribed in fig. 1.1), establishing the basic beat and pace of the game. Improvised slaps and hits, meant to guide the movements of dancers, would be added to this rhythmic pattern at the discretion of the drummer.

Figure 1.1. Standard drum rhythm in *kokomakaku*. RosALIA 1997: 76.

Kokomakaku sticks could be outfitted with thin straps of woven leather shaped into a loop (called *ganchorof*). By slipping the hand through this loop, contestants gained more control over the kokomakaku, and avoided having the stick slip from their grasp. The objective was to hit the opponent on the head with the kokomakaku stick hard enough to draw blood. The first contestant to do so was named winner by the bystanders. Competitions often arose between the different manqueron slave nation groups, and, under those conditions, competitions could become fierce. Winning was a source of pride, and winners gained immediate celebrity status among their communities, who boasted of their champions as "practically invincible" in local hype leading up to competitions, revering winners with "the honorable name of 'stick priest'" (Rosalia 1994). But while these aggressive competitions presented a definite test of athletic ability, in the end, a cunning wit and talent for deception still remained the ultimate weapon required to defeat an opponent.

The music accompanying kokomakaku reflected the familiar binary form. Its opening section was dominated by a lead vocalist, singing special tributes in honor of the individual participants prior to the fight. The purpose of this opening section was to provide a brief biography of each stick fighter, including past fights each had won (or lost), and any special talents or acrobatic moves that set that participant apart from others. Audience members stood quietly at the sidelines, carefully listening to the singer's thoughtful introductions. Once the vocalist finished, the second section commenced, the stick fighters jumping into the circle, the battle now beginning. The lead singer continued in song, but now members of the audience were expected to join in, responding to the main singer in a standard call-and-response manner. Responses offered by the audience served to support the solo singer's words, and inspired kokomakaku participants to maintain high levels of energy and creativity (De Jong 2007).

Uniformly, when New World colonialists sought to maintain control of the growing slave communities, the black martial arts became the focus of censure, with laws instigated to limit their practice. Some of the martial arts dances, like *capoeira*, managed to carry on underground, where they continued to evolve in terms of scope and movement to accommodate the more clandestine settings. Yet, others, like kokomakaku, did not survive; ordinances simply made participation too difficult.

Instead of disappearing altogether, however, kokomakaku assumed new and different forms, a transformation similar to the *kalenda*, whose roots helped establish modern-day calypso. A secular version evolved during the early slave years, which replaced fighting sticks with words. In this version, song texts were used to attack a person's real or supposed shortcomings. Those wanting to even the score might engage a well-respected singer to expressly address the enemy's foibles (usually with satire and sarcasm). Rules of procedure dictated fairness through the equal opportunity for give and take, and those under attack were free to retaliate with their own singers, often presenting even more biting satire. When the battle was all over, attending audiences determined the winner according to whose presentation was the wittiest and most effective. The rules further dictated that when the music ended, the former adversaries should shake hands and redefine their friendship. This new musical performance context acquired the name *Tambú*, its title taken from the accompanying ritual drum, tambú.

A sacred form also emerged, becoming an integral force in the Montamentu religion. Under Angolan command, the Montamentu religion concentrated on the distinctly Angolan religious concept of communing with ancestral spirits. In accordance with Angolan philosophy, Montamentu came to conceive of the human soul as following a cyclic evolutionary pattern (Janzen and MacGaffey 1974: 34). Believers held the notion that although a deceased person's body may be buried, the individual's spirit remains accessible—and an effective source of power and support. From this perspective, death did not constitute an end of one's existence, but rather marked the period of transition when the soul assumes a new dimension of life. Ancestral spirits became sought in Montamentu as vehicles of spiritual guidance and protection; and death, observed more as a kind of freedom, was celebrated as the soul's ascending migration to higher dimensions (Thompson 1983: 108).

The ritual music relied on the binary form continued from kokomakaku. The first section initiated communication with the ancestors, the soloist singing praises not to the stick fighters, but rather to the ancestors. Audience members stood by quietly, carefully listening to the spiritual text. Just as the action of the stick fight occurred in the second part, this form too reserved its ritual action for the second part. Audience members, free to dance in the second section, assumed states of trance, their human bodies temporarily transformed into the spiritual vehicles through which ancestors could communicate with the human world (Honwana 1996, 1997). While the catalyst in kokomakaku had been the drummer, whose improvised slaps and hits guided the stick fighters in battle, the drummer in this sacred ritual held a similar position of authority: it was the drummer who was responsible for mediating between the ancestors and the participants, arousing or terminating states of trance with his mastery of rhythm and vitality of touch.

One particularly inventive Curaçaoan variation on the worship of ancestral spirits was the homage Montamentu paid to the island's original inhabitants—the indigenous Arawak Amerindians. When the Dutch first took possession of Curaçao, the island's population consisted of just thirty-two Spaniards and about five hundred Arawaks, four hundred of which (along with *all* the Spanish) were soon forcibly relocated to Venezuela (Goslinga 1971: 267–269). The hundred or so remaining Arawaks, as G. J. van Grol informs us, refused to serve the Dutch, and were popularly believed to have successfully escaped to Venezuela themselves through Curaçao's twisting system of underground caves (1941–1942: 110). Whatever the actual circumstances of their disappearance, the African slaves idolized the Arawaks for their resistance (ibid.). This is evidenced by the inclusion of Arawak spirits into Montamentu's pantheon, and the religion's elevation of Curaçao's caves to the status of holy sites. By the same token, Venezuela represented a sort of Mt. Olympus to Montamentu believers: a place where the gods and ancestors lived forever, and where, upon their own death, devotees to Montamentu should, themselves, expect to spend eternity (Juliana 1983).

When Portugal gained its independence in 1640, it refocused efforts to reclaim northern Brazil. After years of struggle, the Dutch, in 1654, finally ceded New Holland back to the Portuguese. Since it was the conquest of northern Brazil that originally drew the WIC into the slave trade on a regular basis and on a grand scale, the loss of New Holland might have put an end to Dutch participation in the slave trade. On the contrary, however, the WIC simply shifted its efforts to the illicit *asiento* trade, dealing slave labor specifically to the Spanish mainland colonies. The Dutch regained control over Africa's Cape Coast and other Guinea Coast territories in 1663, leading them to change their trade focus from Angolan to West African slaves. Curaçao became integral to the asiento trade, with the WIC requiring its fleet to "sail ... to Curaçao" upon leaving Africa, and appointing an agent general in Willemstad to serve as liaison between the WIC and Spanish buyers (Rawley 1981: 87). With the advent of the asiento business, the flow of slaves into Curaçao continued to escalate, eventually peaking in the eighteenth century. As the Dutch became more and more involved in the Spanish American trade market, Curaçao became the premiere terminus where Spanish asientists would travel in search of slave labor.

The religion Montamentu and its accompanying music (Tambú) changed under the asiento trade, adopting cultural influences distinct to the island's increased number of West African laborers. Iron instruments were adopted, collectively assuming the title *agan* (the development of the iron instrument is discussed more fully in chapter 3). Iron instruments continue to dominate contemporary performances of the ritual.

West African gods also were integrated into the Montamentu pantheon. Although, admittedly, so vast a territory as West Africa comprised a multiplicity of African nationalities, Paul Mercier points out that centuries of migration, civil wars, and conquest helped to blur the otherwise separate geographic and cultural borders of western Africa. As example, Mercier traces the evolution of certain West African gods and goddesses through specific cultural exchanges initiated during acts of conquest prior to the commencement of the slave trade, where "the deities of the Yoruba had already made their presence felt in Dahomey over hundreds of years. . . . Abomey conquests brought together Yoruba deities already transformed into Ewe and Fon local spirits, in addition to deities from Ketu and Anago Yoruba" (Mercier 1954: 166). From the perspective of such prior cultural exchange, it is easy to see New World creolization as the continuation of an already ongoing process—nothing really new to the African peoples of West Africa. In fact, these enslaved peoples arrived on Curaçao already adept at manipulating their culture in accordance to newly imposed variables—the borrowing and manipulation of deities was already an established tradition with people who might worship the same deity under several different names, or embrace the characteristics of several deities within a single entity. One cultural group might worship a given deity as a male persona, while a nearby community might perceive the same as female. The core similarities that existed within the diverse West African nation groups have been defined by Mintz and Price as "underlying values and beliefs" or "deep structures." These core commonalities enabled West African slaves to more easily transcend immediate circumstances to perceive a deeper shared identity (Mintz and Price 1992: 20–21, 52–53), and allowed them to connect at a basic level on Curaçao. Slavery, for all its horrors and evil, had the effect of reconciling many of the minor differences between these West African societies, their gods and goddesses reunited through the numerous Afro-syncretized religions that emerged throughout the New World. As Montamentu assumed the influences of West African worship, West African gods became sought alongside ancestral spirits as vehicles of guidance and protection.

During the late eighteenth century, slavery took yet another complex turn. In efforts to expand its role in the New World, the WIC established incarceration facilities on Curaçao. While such facilities held prisoners of Spanish, Portuguese, English, and French descent, most were blacks from colonies in South America and other parts of the Caribbean—countries where local politics and plantation economies established unique and divergent creole cultures and traditions. When these black prisoners came to Curaçao, they brought with them the assorted creole cultures of their local New World regions (Postma 1990a: 33–34). Often quartered together with the negotie slaven, this mixture of peoples had a broadening effect on the scope of Curaçaoan creolization. Prisoners from Haiti, Cuba, the Dominican Republic, Brazil, Jamaica, Trinidad, and elsewhere were represented, bringing to Curaçao a unique sophistication of influence. Montamentu was suddenly impacted with a number of syncretic religions from each area, including Haitian *Vodou,* Brazilian *Candomblé,* and Dominican *Santería.*

Some of the black New World prisoners remained on Curaçao, assuming membership in the manqueron community, where they retained their own set of deities. A continued lack of interest in indigenous beliefs among the Dutch allowed the creole prisoners to share their New World syncretized religions amongst themselves and with the Curaçaoan manquerons.

Montamentu, already a refuge for displaced African gods, now absorbed the creole deities into a rapidly expanding pantheon which accepted Vodou *lwas* and Santería *orishas* as rapidly as *Eshu, Shango,* and a host of other deities from the Gulf of Guinea. Because each creole community shared its own versions of gods like *Eshu* and *Shango,* duplication—sometimes triplication—of gods took place. Montamentu did not discriminate against any deities, explaining why at least four separate *Eshu* gods are present in modern-day Montamentu. Included, in addition to the *Eshu* deity acknowledged by Curaçao's current manqueron community, are found *Legba* (borrowed from Haitian Vodou), *Ellegba* (from the Dominican Santería religion), and *Ellegua* (appropriated from Cuban Santería). As explained by several Tambú ritual leaders, these do not so much represent different aspects of the same god as they represent independent deities able to coexist, each characterized by distinctly different Caribbean or African origins (Yuchi, personal communication, November 3, 1995; Wendel, personal communication, November 3, 1995; Alwin, personal communication, December 29, 2001).

This duplication and triplication of gods separated Montamentu from other Afro-syncretized religions in the New World. Vodou and Santería may have embraced variants of the same god, yet never were these variants considered anything but separate personality traits of the same deity. As example, Vodou names *Legba* and *Kafou Legba* as the trickster god; *Legba* is benevolent, while *Kafou Legba* is malevolent. Although characteristically different, *Legba* and *Kafou Legba* are not regarded as separate entities. Rather, they represent the different personalities (and functions) of the same *lwa* (Deren 1972; Desmangles 1992; Métraux 1972).

Already a medley of different cultural influences, Montamentu blossomed again as it adopted practices distinct to the New World creole religions introduced by prisoners. For example, the religious leader in Montamentu assumed the title of *Obeah-man* or *-woman,* a label generally associated with spiritual heads from the syncretized religions of the English Caribbean. In a similar vein, the use of symbolic, spiritual drawings for magical purposes also became integrated into Montamentu. Called *Veve,* a term borrowed from Haitian Vodou, the emblematic drawings were carefully traced on the ground, or sometimes drawn in cornmeal, coffee grounds, or burnt ashes near entranceways before Montamentu worshipers arrived for services. It was believed symbolic motifs constituting images of the specific deities and ancestral spirits to be invoked might establish a link between the human and the supernatural worlds (Rosalia, personal communication, September 29, 1995).

Still another evolutionary turn in Montamentu occurred when pious European colonialists came to the Dutch expressing an interest in purchasing Africans already indoctrinated into Christianity. Seizing the opportunity of adding monetary value to their human commodity, the WIC obliged its paying customers by imposing religious training on all negotie slaven. Uninterested in converting the Africans themselves, the Dutch commissioned priests from nearby Venezuela to travel to the island to indoctrinate negotie slaven with regular mass services and religious education. Later, the WIC went so far as to authorize Catholic missionaries to accompany its slavers to Africa so that the indoctrinization process might commence immediately upon capture (Goslinga 1985: 370).

Although the Dutch did not encourage Catholic training among the manquerons, their continuing disinterest was a green light for priests to minister to the manqueron community as well. Writes Charles Goslinga, "So long as the [indoctrination of blacks] could be safely ignored . . . Dutch officials were satisfied" (1985: 369). Venezuelan priests took up permanent and semi-permanent residence on the island, and at least one, a Father Theodorus Browuer (who relocated to Curaçao in 1776), conducted his sermons in the island's creole language (Brada 1950: 32).

Cultural flexibility had important Old World precedents—the concept of a single main God with a pantheon of lesser deities was shared by numerous African cultures (Thompson 1983; Mercier 1954). Furthermore, owing to wars and years of intermarriage, African religions tended often to share deities who, known by different names, sometimes became composite gods—embodying a diversity of powers and attributes chosen from other cultural sources; similarly, a deity assigned a male persona within one national context might be worshiped as a female within another (ibid.). When Venezuelan priests distributed woodcuts and lithographs of the Catholic saints, manquerons immediately recognized striking parallels connecting "Christian figures and powers to the forces of their own ancient deities" (Thompson 1983: 16). Quietly appropriating the saints while continuing to honor traditional African deities, the manquerons "could outwardly abide by the religious properties of the Catholics who surrounded them, but they covertly practiced a system of thought that was a creative reorganization of their own traditional religion" (ibid.). As can be seen, rather than spelling

the end of Montamentu, Catholic indoctrination had quite the opposite effect—followers of Montamentu not only embraced Catholicism, but added
the saints to their existing pantheon of deities. Furthermore, Montamentu
adopted the Catholic ritual calendar, infusing into existing ceremonies references to both the familiar African deities and the names of saints. It is
important to remember that the teachings of Catholicism were not entirely
new to most negotie slaven or manquerons, as they had already learned
about the religion, and had included Catholic-inspired rituals within the
New World counterparts of Vodou and Santería. What was new, however,
was the formal training they were now receiving.

In 1795, Curaçao witnessed its first major slave revolt. Testimony to the
creole influence on Curaçao, this revolt was inspired in part by the stories
shared by Haitian prisoners about their country's 1792 revolution. In fact,
at the head of the Curaçaoan revolt was a French creole slave, Louis Mercier, and a Curaçaoan-born slave, Tula, who assumed the name of Riguad,
after General Benoit Joseph Riguad of Haiti. Initially, the revolt involved
about seventy manquerons from the Knip plantation (located along the island's southwestern coast). However, within a few days of its launch, over a
thousand slaves from western Curaçao became involved (Benjamin 2002:
75–76). Although Tula and Mercier had carefully organized the revolt, both
failed to take Curaçao's very even topography into consideration. Vastly different than mountainous Haiti, the island of Curaçao offered the rebels nowhere to hide. As a result, the Curaçaoan revolt ended about a month after it
began, with the majority of slaves forced back to work, and its twenty-nine
leaders executed.

Soon after the revolt, the Dutch tightened their control of the manqueron community. In an effort to curb future revolts, they issued ordinances enforcing Catholic training among the manquerons. Venezuelan
priests consequentially were summoned to conduct Mass services for both
the negotie slaven and the manquerons. Montamentu and performances of
Tambú were officially banned by the church and the state. Manquerons responded by taking both Montamentu and Tambú underground, where they
actually gained strength as symbols of resistance and empowerment. With
the ban, the manqueron community was forced to redefine its presence on
Curaçao, and was obliged to reestablish its cultural boundaries.

When emancipation eventually freed Curaçao's slaves in 1863, the situation initiated renewed concerns among Dutch colonialists about losing their
dominant voice in governing the island. Rejoining forces with the Catholic

Church, the Dutch organized an aggressive campaign to abolish Monta-mentu, with Tambú used as the focus for the attack. As discussed in further detail in chapter 3, Catholic priests were not above using the pulpit to de-liver weekly monologues against the perceived "evil character" of Tambú, advising parishioners their very souls might be at risk (Juliana 1987, 1990). To further their efforts to thwart Afro-Curaçaoans' affiliation with Tambú, Catholic priests decried Montamentu, instigating the epithet *Brua* to refer to its followers, condemning Tambú as an "African pastime" meant for "people who are unintelligent—the black people of Africa" (Juliana 1990: 2). In sup-port, the Dutch officials instigated numerous ordinances outlawing Tambú activity, under which public Tambú dancing (when done without a permit) remains an unlawful act.

While previous regulation of Montamentu and Tambú had the effect of strengthening the culturally risky forms, metamorphosing them into tools of resistance and empowerment, this new onslaught of legal and religious sanctions pushed Montamentu and Tambú so far underground that neither reappeared with strength or authority. Understandably, Afro-Curaçaoans found religious disapproval, legal repression, and social scrutiny worrisome. Many, finding participation too risky, made the difficult decision to aban-don their association with Montamentu and Tambú. Those brave enough to confront the consequences remained connected—though only in guarded secrecy.

Creolization was a means through which distinct cultural histories and traditions were born, and through which imagined and remembered com-munities were conceived. Montamentu provides a first-rate metaphor for creolization. Like Afro-Caribbean culture itself, it came to experience con-stant renewal, "not created once and then left to its own momentum," but rather "constantly produced and reproduced, pruned for a clear profile, and softened to absorb revitalizing elements" (Bell 1992: 7). A by-product of numerous traditions, Montamentu emerged at the interface between past and present, to represent "the in-between" or "third space" separating Af-rica and the New World (Bhabha 1994). For the ethnographer, Montamentu provides valuable records, full of clues of summoned gods, musical rhythms, and song texts that invoke explanation of, or argument to, the principles professed by memory. For the Afro-Caribbean people, Montamentu stands as a complex source of empowerment, providing connections to individu-ally remembered pasts, while traversing the rocky thoroughfare of a fre-quently changing future.

Told through the Fierce Rhythms of the Drum

Kontá pa e Ritmonan Furioso di su Barí

Materials, including both the music itself, and the ritual complexes from
which it is derived, represent the primary cultural documents within
which crucial evidence may be encoded. —KAY SHELEMAY

The term *Tambú* is used today interchangeably to define the specific drum
instrument, the dance, the song, and the occasion itself. Through the recent
centuries, the sacred role of Tambú has been eclipsed by its secular role,
where Tambú is tantamount to an oral newspaper, a medium for the documentation of local news and gossip and for its dissemination to the island's
distant corners. Whatever its function, sacred or secular, however, Tambú
maintains the same performance practices.

Typically, Tambú is announced by a lead singer, called *pregon*, who calls
people to the ceremony with a short, declamatory *a capella* introduction,
called *deklarashon introduktorio*. This *deklarashon introduktorio* signals to
the chorus (*coro*), accompanying musicians, and audience participants that
a Tambú is about to commence. Its purpose also is to establish the tonal
center for the music that will follow, to introduce the basic melodic and
rhythmic motives of the upcoming song, and to specify, through text, the
title or plot of the impending Tambú. The Tambú that follows may be said

to reflect a binary form, consisting of two main sections: the *habrí* ("open") and *será* ("closed"). Habrí is always heard first, and is always followed by the será section. Although the two sections can be repeated as often as the pregon desires, they are always presented as a pair—never singly, and never out of order. An optional coda with the pregon restating the Tambú title or plot provides finality.

At the heart of Tambú beats a single drum, which is known as *tambú* or *barí* ("barrel"). While the modern barí is made from pieces of wood glued into a cylinder shape, during the early years it was constructed from a hollowed-out tree trunk, its opening covered with animal skin. When governmental forces and Catholic policies pushed the Tambú underground, it became necessary to have a lighter, more portable drum—one easily moved between secret locations, and quickly hidden in case of discovery. For a time, simple household items—including tables and chairs—were transformed into barí drums.

Another expedient drum substitute, known as the *kalbas den tobo* ("calabash in a tub"), made specific use of wooden wash tubs borrowed from the servants who used them for washing clothes. The tub was filled about three-quarters full of water, and on top was floated a large calabash half. With the tub serving as a resonator, the calabash was hit with two pieces of wood, which had small pieces of cloth tied to their ends. Since the barí produced a loud, percussive sound, the much softer, somewhat indistinct timbre of the kalbas den tobo produced a muffled and quiet sound that enabled Tambú events to remain secretive. The kalbas den tobo, however, caught on only as an occasional substitute in Tambú. Rather, the instrument assumed prominence within another Afro-Curaçaoan ritual—*Seú*, a harvest ritual that emerged among the *manqueron* slaves. On Curaçao, where rainfall was infrequent and crop-growing was difficult, proprietors provided small plots of land on plantation grounds to the manquerons, where they were expected to harvest their own food. Seú emerged as a New World ritual used by the slave community to ensure successful harvests, performed prior to planting and again at harvest time. The kalbas den tobo was central to the ritual (De Jong 2005).

During the years of colonialism, trees had become increasingly scarce on Curaçao. For centuries, the indigenous Arawak Amerindians (*Caiqutios*) had traditionally planted and maintained uniform groves around their villages. With the entrance of European colonialists, that tradition had died, as did the prospect of new trees. A new type of barí was soon to appear though—one constructed from wooden boards gleaned from old fruit and vegetable boxes, and carefully cut and glued together to form a cylinder. Sheep skin was then stretched over the top, after being made smooth and hairless through a process known as *cotie*, involving frequent soaks in a mixture of chalk and water. A band of tin nailed to the drum itself ensured its circular design, and the spanned skin was held in place by two rings called *hopps*. This construction technique continues to dominate the building of contemporary barí drums. (Figures 2.1–2.4 provide a photographic series depicting the making of the barí. Sherwin "Pincho" Anita, famous on the island for his talents as a Tambú band leader and singer, is also well known for making some of the finest Tambú drums. He is pictured in each of these photos, showing the process of making a drum he later sold to a client.)

The making of a modern barí (2.1–2.4)

The modern barí is considered a spiritual instrument, even within secular contexts. Each barí is believed uniquely endowed with an essential life-force or spirit. Montamentu devotees eagerly await the first soundings of a newly built drum, hopeful to discern within its unique timbre the voice of a deceased loved one. At sacred Tambú performances the drummer, called *tambúrero* (traditionally male), assumes the role of medium between the spiritual realm and barí, his music imparting messages from beyond to believers who approach in turn. Because each barí houses a unique spirit, each new drum is ceremoniously christened, and referred to thereafter by its specific name. Barís presumed to house the spirits of specifically known individuals adopt the deceased's name. Further personification is projected onto the barí drum by way of numerous phrases and expressions coined to represent the barí's presumed needs and proclivities, including *Tambú ta pida sanger* ("Tambú asks for blood") and *Tambú ta hik* ("Tambú has the hiccups") (Rosalia 1997: 56).

The catalyst of every Tambú ceremony is the tambúrero, whose mastery of rhythm and vitality of touch mediate between gods and spirits, and the Tambú participants. A talented tambúrero will use the barí to "speak" with what one Curaçaoan drummer called "*Hopi frenesí!*" ("much frenzy") (Pincho, personal communication, December 29, 2001). Gifted not only with a great sense of rhythm but also with exceptional stamina (as Tambú events may typically last for many hours), the tambúrero may arouse or terminate a state of trance among the audience. Sustaining rhythmic melodies and

Figure 2.1. Photograph of the drum frame. PHOTO BY AUTHOR.

passages to hypnotic effect, a capable drummer controls the event. Head thrown back, eyes shut, face strained, the tambúrero performs as though serenely possessed. Yet in reality this is hardly so: a skilled tambúrero is the master of his art, and is specifically trained to withstand the temptation of trance.[1]

1. It may be mentioned that contemporary Tambú drums continue to be played only by men in Curaçao.

Figure 2.2. Photograph of the *hopps,* used to bind the drum frame. PHOTO BY AUTHOR.

On the other hand, an inexperienced tambúrero whose fingers have not yet mastered the rhythmic intricacies of Tambú can easily cast dancers into confusion and directly hinder the goals of the event. The artistry of the tambúrero is more than an inherent talent; an extended apprenticeship begins early. The transference of knowledge between established tambúreros and novices takes years. Young boys aspiring to become tambúreros will be taught basic techniques during ceremony interludes. Older boys already skilled in the basics will be allowed to assume the stage at the end of a ceremony in order to play for the last few dancers after the now exhausted professional tambúrero has left the ceremony. Seeking the approval of onlookers, neophytes take great pride in showing off their skills to the public. Today

Figure 2.3. Photograph showing the *cotie* process (soaking of the sheep skin). PHOTO BY AUTHOR.

Figure 2.4. Photograph showing the skinning of the drum. PHOTO BY AUTHOR.

there exist several Tambú bands on Curaçao that have developed into arenas for promising young musicians. Rene Rosalia (and his *Grupo Trinchera*) and Pincho (of *Pincho y su Grupo*), both dedicated to the preservation of Curaçaoan culture, welcome adolescents to attend rehearsals and to learn the established Tambú traditions. Through Rosalia, Pincho, and others, Tambú has successfully acquired and maintained a young audience, and the legacy has been passed to subsequent generations. Although becoming a tambúrero may not be a lucrative profession, it still garners a certain amount of prestige and some fear among modern Curaçaoans. "To be a tambúrero means you are powerful in mind and the spirit," explains one Curaçaoan (Franklyn, personal communication, August 10, 1997). "I admire the tambúrero," explains another. "But I also fear him. If you see a great lion in a jungle—the 'king of the jungle' they call him—you can admire his strength; but you are careful not to upset him. He might just come by and take a big bite from your ass when you are not looking" (Randall, personal communication, August 13, 2000).

While there is only one barí involved in Tambú, there may be numerous iron instruments. Known collectively as *herú*, they are an important accessory. Together, the iron instruments initiate a polyrhythmic backdrop, each

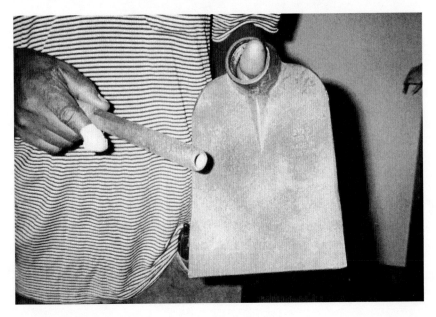

Figure 2.5. Close-up of *chapi* instrument. PHOTO BY AUTHOR.

Figures 2.6. Photograph of Tambú drummer, with *chapi* musicians, taken at rehearsal on Curaçao (2001). Photo by author.

providing a different pitch to create cross-rhythmic harmonies. Although the rhythmic component is certainly pronounced in the role of the iron, the herú also serve to enhance the Tambú melody. There have been five basic types of herú, although when iron instruments are not available, a pair of scissors, biscuit tins, even kerosene cans make expedient substitutes. The earliest herú was the *agan di tres pida* ("iron in three pieces"), consisting of two thick iron bars and one long iron tube. The tube, split down the side and open at each end, was held between the knees, its split side facing up. The *agan di tres pida* was played by a seated individual who struck the tube with

Figure 2.7. Close-up of Tambú drummer. PHOTO BY AUTHOR.

an iron bar in each hand, producing tones and pitches according to where the tube was hit, and by which of the two bars. A second type of herú is known as the *agan di dos pida* ("iron in two pieces"). *Agan di dos pida* involved the same split iron tube used with the *agan di tres pida*, but just a single iron bar. What the single striking bar sacrifices in terms of tonal variation, it makes up for in freeing the herú performer to dance and move among the others gathered. A third type of herú, called *triangel*, involved bending an iron bar into a triangular shape. Held one-handedly in a manner allowing optimum tone, the *triangel* was struck with a second iron bar. A fourth herú type is the *wiri*, which involves a serrated piece of iron over which a thin iron bar can be scraped to produce a raspy timbre. Today, the *wiri* remains a common accompaniment to the Antillean waltz (De Jong 2003a). The fifth and final type of herú is the *chapi*, born of field expediency during the days of slavery, and still popular in modern Tambú. The chapi, literally the metal end of a common garden hoe, produces a loud, uniquely high-pitched tone when struck with an iron bar. (Figure 2.5 provides a close-up picture of the chapi instrument.) The chapi is the most commonly used herú in contemporary Tambú (both sacred and secular). Rene Rosalia suggests Curaçaoans borrowed the use of the chapi from the Dahomean people's *oggán*—also built from a garden hoe. The major difference being that the oggán was strictly used in ceremonies in adoration of the saints; the chapi, on the other hand, is a symbol of life and fertility (1997: 41).

While many Afro-based music groups employ iron instruments in the role of timekeeper, the herú assume a wider role in Tambú. They contribute melodic and rhythmic lines (in both the habrí and será sections) that are both independent from and interdependent with other instruments. In the opening habrí section, the herú are indispensable as the basic timekeeper, whose repetitive phrases offer a rhythmic foundation over which the barí drummer can improvise (a photograph of a Tambú drummer with accompanying chapi musicians appears in figure 2.6; a close-up photograph of a Tambú drummer appears in figure 2.7). During the habrí section, performance protocol dictates that the herú serve as timekeepers while the barí drummer is free to improvise. In the será, however, these roles are reversed. Now the barí is expected to maintain the downbeat while the herú provides quick, repetitive triplet phrases interspersed with episodes of improvisation. (Traditional herú and barí rhythms, for both habrí and será sections, are transcribed in figures 2.8 through 2.11.)

Figure 2.8. Musical transcription of the standard rhythm performed by the *barí* during the *habrí* section of Tambú.

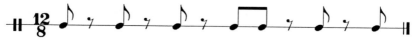

Figure 2.9. Musical transcription of the standard rhythm performed by the *herú* during the *habrí* section of Tambú.

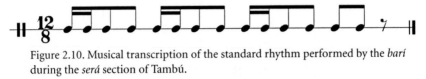

Figure 2.10. Musical transcription of the standard rhythm performed by the *barí* during the *será* section of Tambú.

Figure 2.11. Musical transcription of the standard rhythm performed by the *herú* during the *será* section of Tambú.

Tambú's crowning musical texture is applied vocally by the pregon and coro. Following the short *deklarashon introduktorio,* the pregon introduces the main text and melody of the Tambú song in the habrí section. Here, the pregon communicates the performance-specific Tambú message while the audience and chorus keep quiet, paying their undivided attention, careful not to miss even a word. Dancing, hand clapping, or anything else considered distracting is never allowed during the habrí, and although pregons are known to personalize the habrí with subtle vocal ornamentation, they are careful not to interrupt the melodic flow or obfuscate the text—such modifications, should they occur, are generally mild.

The pregon controls the structure of the Tambú, and decides when the habrí ends and the next section, the será, begins. With a wave of the hand, the pregon cuts the habrí off at the proper moment, and, through a vocal call (called *yamada*), combined often with accompanying hand movements, signals the commencement of the será. During the será section, the coro responds to the pregon in a standard call-and-response manner. Responses offered by the coro serve as *afirmashon* ("affirmation") of the pregon's words, and inspire the solo singer's further creativity. Fervor often intensifies during the será section, and builds to exciting climaxes. As protocol dictates, a coro member or onlooking participant wanting to assume the role of solo vocalist will put a hand over the pregon's mouth in an action known as *pidi boka* ("asking for mouth"). People generally attend Tambú events with the purpose of hearing their favorite pregon perform, and should an outsider succeed in assuming the solo role, he or she will face a very critical audience indeed. The process, known as *e don pa por manda* ("to throw words"), distinguishes the talented pregon and coro from the amateur.

If an audience sees a favorite pregon tiring, they will often hand the singer money in hopes the donation will motivate the singer to continue.

However, if the pregon becomes too exhausted, the drummer will immediately stop playing, thus giving the singer the opportunity to take a break. In
this instance, a coro or audience participant is expected to take over—generally not an easy position to fill!

During the será, audience members are free to participate through
hand clapping (called *brassa*) and foot stomping (called *pisotea*). Both the
brassa and pisotea are equally vital to the Tambú event. In fact, when the
herú was abandoned for a time during the early years of the ban on Tambú,
the brassa and pisotea assumed a more significant importance, often used
as replacements for the iron instruments.

Dancing is done with one heel grounded in place, while participants
utilize the toes of the free foot to stomp rhythmically. On wooden or cement floors, the sounds of the pisotea were amplified. If pisotea seems less
a part of modern Tambú than brassa, it is because most modern Tambú
events are held outdoors, and foot stomping is generally audible only when
performed on wooden dance floors. But as Elis Juliana points out, whether
or not the pisotea is heard does not limit the visual beauty it offers the
Tambú dance (1983). However, such physical movement not only provides
a good deal of visual effect (Rosalia calls it "polymovement"), but also en-
hances the already complex será rhythm line. Audiences also accentuate the
downbeat through hand clapping—more than mere responses by spectators, the hand claps became vital to the musical performance of Tambú
as well, serving to add another rhythmic dimension to an already dense
texture. The performance of brassa requires one hand be held outstretched,
fingers and palm held upwards, while the other hand hits it smartly before
springing backwards. This is then repeated in reverse, with the hands exchanging roles.

The rhythms established through brassa and pisotea are transcribed in
figures 2.12 and 2.13.

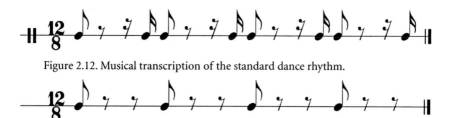

Figure 2.12. Musical transcription of the standard dance rhythm.

Figure 2.13. Musical transcription of the standard hand-clapping rhythm.

Tambú dance carries its own strict rules of etiquette. It may be danced individually or in pairs. If danced with a partner, dancers are explicitly forbidden to touch while dancing together—a rule that is maintained among all the Tambú types, sacred or secular. There is, however, one exception to this: should a woman feel her male partner begin to crowd her dance space, she is allowed to gently push him away as a sign to remind him to keep his distance. An additional rule dictates that the couple should face one another at all times. Should a man on the sidelines decide he wants to dance, he may approach a couple through the process known as *pidi skina* ("asking for a corner"). Only men are allowed to approach couples on the dance floor, and a man must make his advance on bended knees, his arms outstretched. Gently he may step in front of the man and assume a place on the dance floor. During the maneuver, he is required to ask *"Skina bari?"* ("May I have a piece of this dance?"), or *"Dunami un sanka i mei?"* ("May I have half of this dance?"). If the already-engaged male partner accepts the *pidi skina*, he will acknowledge the advance by stepping aside. Otherwise, he will answer the request with the phrase, *"Bai bolbe!"* ("Go away and come back later!"). At this point the man asking for the *pidi skina* should quietly leave for a time, and return later in the evening. Occasionally, though, a confrontational game called *trankamentu* ensues, involving playful pushing and shoving between the men. Meanwhile, the woman is left either to dance alone or to retreat to the sidelines of the dance floor. Should the men get carried away with the battle, the *trankamentu* may escalate into a *kokomakaku*, the confrontational game fought with sticks. At the first signs of a kokomakaku, the dance floor is cleared as Tambú drummers take charge of the stick fight. Onlookers head for the sidelines as the tambúrero assumes command, controlling the action with hits and slaps that could inspire players to more intense levels of interaction, or calm them should the action become too heated.

A musical analysis of a Tambú is provided below. The song, titled *"Rebeldia na Bandabou"* ("Rebellion at Bandabou"), comprises a form typical of Tambú, and, therefore, is a good example to use for discussion. "Rebeldia na Bandabou" describes the revolt from the Afro-Curaçaoan perspective—naming the plantation (Landhuis Knip is located in the Bandabou region of the island) and individuals involved (including slave heroes Tula and Bastiaan Carpata), as well as tracing the route the rebellion followed. This particular Tambú is frequently performed by the group *Grupo Trinchera*, which, under the direction of Rene Rosalia, has become a vehicle for performing and preserving early Tambú—Tambú uncovered and researched by Rosalia himself. "Rebeldia na Bandabou" reflects Tambú's role as memory keeper. The events of slavery were common themes in Tambú. For their own part, the slaves were unable to leave written accounts of their side of the story, and instead documented their versions through Tambú.

Text to "Rebeldia na Bandabou":

Rebeldia na Bandabou	**Rebellion at Bandabou**

[Deklarashon introduktorio]

| Diesshete di agosto ora bel a bati | August seventeenth when the bell rang |

[Habrí—Pregon]

Henter Kenepa den tenshon.	There was much tension at Knip [plantation]
Katibunan a disidi ku t'awe,	The slaves have decided today,
Kos ta termina.	Things will end.
Katibunan a disidi ku t'awe:	Slaves have decided today:
Libertad ta start.	Liberty will start.
Ora bel a zona	When the bell sounded
Henter Kenepa den tenshon.	There was much tension at Knip.
Katibunan a reuni,	The slaves have reunited,
I huntu nan a disidi,	And together have decided,
Ku awe tin rebeldia na Bandabou.	Today there will be rebellion at Bandabou.

[Será—Coro with Pregon]

Rebeldia na Bandabou.	Rebellion at Bandabou.
Na kabes tin un kapitan,	At the head there is a captain,
Rebeldia na Bandabou.	Rebellion at Bandabou.
Kaptan Tula ta na mando.	Captain Tula is in command.
Rebeldia na Bandabou.	Rebellion at Bandabou.
Na su lado Pedro Wacao.	At his side is Pedro Wacao.

Rebeldia na Bandabou.	Rebellion at Bandabou.
Luis Mercer tambe ta lucha.	Luis Mercer is also fighting.
Rebeldia na Bandabou.	Rebellion at Bandabou.
Un djis den banda ata Sablika.	Just at the side there is Sablika.
Rebeldia na Bandabou.	Rebellion at Bandabou.
Hombernan den rebeldia,	Men in rebellion,
Rebeldia na Bandabou.	Rebellion at Bandabou.
Muhenan tambe ta lucha.	Women also in fight.

[*Habrí—Pregon*]

Tokado di mi tobo ban kumi	Tambú player come with me
Pa Porto Marie!	To Porto Marie!
Ban kumi na	Come with me to
Seru di Neger!	Niger hill!
Barikada na seri Neger!	Barricade at Niger hill!
Pader Schink ke kibra e lucha	Pastor Schink wants to break up the fight
Ku Beibel of Bayonete.	With the Bible or bayonet.
Libertad pa todo el mundo!	Liberty for everybody!
Kibra e bel pe stop di zona.	Break the bell to stop it from sounding.
Kibra e bel pe stop di zona.	Break the bell to stop it from sounding.
Ay ma, rebeldia na Bandabou!	Oh mama, rebellion at Bandabou!

As revealed in the musical transcription (fig. 2.14a and b), the text of the *a cappella* introduction (*deklarashon introduktorio*) preceding "Rebeldia na Bandabou" ("Rebellion at Bandabou") immediately and clearly communicates to the audience the purpose and intention of the Tambú to follow (i.e., "*Diesshete di Agosto ora bel a bati*" refers to the date of the revolt—August 17). This introductory text moves Tambú participants to commence applause, and prepares them for the Tambú. Shouting its title in unison, participants in turn demonstrate understanding and their readiness to take part. As chapi beats signal the close of the *deklarashon introduktorio*, the Tambú moves into full swing.

The secondary and tertiary purposes of the *deklarashon introduktorio*—the establishment of a tonal center around which the diatonic coloring distinguishing the Tambú then revolves, and the introduction of basic motives that will comprise the song melody itself—are evidenced by the *deklarashon introduktorio* preceding "Rebeldia na Bandabou." In this example, the Aeolian mode is established, and two central motives are introduced. The first, a descending six-note motive, provides closure to the opening phrase of the introduction, and later, in extended form, comprises the habrí melody. This motive ultimately evolves within the coro refrain heard in the será section. The second important motive is intervallic—a perfect fourth (G–C)—and is repeated several times during the habrí, each time with increasing urgency. Resolution, when it arrives at the close of the section, is punctuated by the recurrence of the original descending motive again, signifying closure.

The Tambú is distinguished by a rhythmic counterpoint where the percussion, singers, and audience interlock in varied patterns of two against three. The herú and barí provide the triplet pulse, transcribed by the author in a $^{12}/_8$ meter (see figs. 2.8 through 2.11). The pregon, and later the coro, transcribed by the author in $^4/_4$ (see fig. 2.14a and b), shift between the triple and duple, which establishes the complex musical tapestry defining the Tambú art form. When the brassa and pisotea enter during the será section, they serve to accentuate the downbeat. As a result, the hand clapping and dance rhythms can be transcribed in either $^{12}/_8$ or $^4/_4$, signaling that participants may assume musical partnership with both the percussionists and singers.

While Tambú's binary form connotes a definite structural symmetry, its actual phraseology seldom maintains a uniformity of length. Instead, asymmetrical phrases generate pulse rhythms that more precisely conform to the rhythmic speech patterns of Papiamento, with Tambú's intervallic relationships and modal melodies reflecting the common tonal inflections of spoken Papiamento. "Rebeldia na Bandabou," therefore, offers a fine example of the irregular phraseology, intervallic relationships, and diatonic melodic progressions Tambú is known for—its symmetrical binary form notwithstanding.

Through the centuries, Tambú has experienced alternating periods of acceptance and repression from the island's dominant minority society—the Dutch. Periodic bouts of repression, both by the Dutch and Catholic

Rebeldia na Bandabou

Figure 2.14a and b. Musical transcription of the *habrí* and (opening) *será* sections of *"Rebeldia na Bandabou."* TRANSCRIPTION BY THE AUTHOR, TAKEN DURING A LIVE PERFORMANCE BY THE TAMBÚ ENSEMBLE *GRUPO TRINCHERA,* JANUARY 2002.

Church, however, have not succeeded in wiping out Tambú, and in retrospect have only served its evolution and tenacity. By fulfilling different social functions (sacred and secular), distinct Tambú types emerged, their meaning assumed in accordance with the diverging needs and interests of the society. Although the Tambú itself has survived in altered contexts, its distinguishing patterns of structural form, musicality, and choreography have remained intact.

In fact, the exact same rhythms and dance patterns used to invoke spiritual deities are used at Tambú parties (where the ritual music is performed as entertainment). As outwardly surprising as this may seem, Samuel Floyd reminds, "In traditional African culture, there was no formal distinction between the sacred and the profane realms of life, or between the material and the spiritual" (1995: 15). In fact, "there was in traditional Africa no word for 'religion' because the Africans' religion permeated and was the basis for all aspects of life, including education, politics, harvesting, hunting, homemaking, and community welfare" (ibid.). In similar fashion, then, Tambú interweaves the sacred and secular aspects of Afro-Curaçaoan life.

From this perspective, the modern Tambú maintains its sense of tradition, despite transformation in meaning. Tambú's continued reliance on a binary structure, distinct instrumentation, set patterns of barí and herú rhythms, and customary performance rules for both musicians and dancers, all stand as constant references to history, informing the ethos of a former time, reflecting "the historical continuum from which [they] emerged" (Shelemay 1980: 233). They make possible the expected effect of Tambú as historical document, and operate as the essential elements that mediate both the experience and the representation of memory. With pieces of the island's early African heritage and New World history still perceivable, all Curaçaoans attending a Tambú event, be it sacred or secular, are provided an opportunity to realign themselves with the memories of a distant past.

The Laws Couldn't Keep Tambú Away.
The Church Couldn't Keep Tambú Away.

Leinan No Por a Tene Tambú Lew.
Misa No Por a Tene Tambú Lew.

Art should be recognized as a major and integral part of the transaction that engenders political behavior. —MURRAY EDELMAN

As already stated, during the early slavery years Tambú was allowed to evolve without much interference. Early Dutch interests were focused almost entirely on trade and profits, and the personal lives of *manquerons* were at first of little interest to the slaveholders. As the Jamaican governor of 1694 aptly observed in describing the Hollanders on Curaçao: "Jesus Christ is good, but trade is better" (Hamelberg 1694: 107). This helps to explain how Tambú managed to catch on quickly and spread rapidly among the manqueron community.

Among Tambú's main purposes during slavery was its role as accompaniment to Montamentu, its rhythms and dances performed as vehicles for conjuring the arrival of ancestors and deities, many of whom found duplication (and triplication) on Curaçao. Montamentu's propensity for duplicated gods stemmed in part from the religion's unusual rules of possession. Unlike most other Afro-syncretized Caribbean rituals, Montamentu's invocation of specific gods and spirits was not limited to performing the specific musical rhythms and dances unique to the individual entity. In Tambú, for example, while events could be performed in honor of a particular deity, "all deities [were] welcome." According to one respected Tambú leader, "It is the spirit world that makes the decision [regarding] which deities will arrive. [The spirit world] is best qualified to make that decision" (Yuchi, personal communication, November 3, 1995). Which gods arrive, how many gods attend, how long the gods will stay—these are all decisions made at the discretion of the gods themselves.

Tambú's binary structure specifically enabled the spirit world to be accessed directly by way of the Montamentu ritual itself. The preliminary of summoning *Eshu* (the gatekeepers) to throw open the gates to the spirit world—proper protocol in other Afro-syncretized rituals—was not mandatory to open Montamentu proceedings. It was believed heaven's gates were pried open not by *Eshu,* but by the very ritual performance itself. Tambú's first section (*habrí*) had this effect, and with the gates so opened, the second part of Tambú (the *será*) witnessed the gods' and spirits' arrival.

In the sacred Tambú, then, the habrí section was used to present a formal invocation to the gods and spirits—a request for their help and guidance within the human realm. The point of contact between the spiritual and temporal worlds was the beginning of the será. At this point, the *Obeah-man* or *-woman* serving as guide to spiritual possession entered the spirit world to summon the presence of the deity whose advice was being sought. The Obeah-man or -woman, having achieved possession, would empower other participants to enter spiritual possession themselves. Dancers' repetitive foot-stomp rhythms helped induce a group trance. In the words of cultural historian Elis Juliana, dancers "let the whole body weight fall on the left foot without bending the knee. Because the left knee is not bent, it would absorb the shock" (1983: 14). This high-impact dance caused participants "to lose contact with reality. In other words, when the shock would leave the left foot, it would take away all the pain, and the bitterness. With the Tambú, then, you could dance away all your hurt" (ibid.).

Funerals presented a second important occasion where Tambú emerged vital. Given the Afro-Curaçaoan proclivity for ancestral veneration, it is not surprising that the funeral became a critical part of culture. A traditional funeral involved an eight-day (and nine-night) cycle of prayer, during which time friends and relatives shared stories about the deceased. To early Afro-Curaçaoans, when an individual died, the body was buried but the spirit remained vital. From this perspective, death was not the end of one's existence, but rather the moment one's soul transitioned to another dimension. Friends and relatives of the deceased joined others in a long procession past the body. They shouted, chanted, sang to Tambú rhythms, through which it was believed the souls of the deceased might successfully travel to Venezuela, the "promised land" where they could reconnect with the deities and spend eternity with the ancestors. At burial, another procession formed to file past the grave site, each participant throwing in three rocks as a last tribute to the deceased, all done to the accompaniment of Tambú. Thereafter, the procession moved on to the home of the deceased for a ritual washing of the hands, and to offer their final condolences to the family. Participating in funerals was considered "an obligatory ritual," Rosalia writes, adding that "not taking part in the ritual would make you an enemy of the family and of the community" (1997: 105).

In addition to igniting communication with the spiritual world, traditional Tambú was also used at the event *Manda Fuku Bai*—performed for purposes of driving away the *fuku* ("bad spirits") through singing, dancing, and the burning of incense. Although performing Tambú for reasons of ridding fuku could be scheduled anytime during the year, the most popular occasion was during New Year's, when it was particularly hoped Tambú would chase away last year's fuku and initiate good fortune for the coming year.

A fourth Tambú type was created to bring rain. As already noted, the Dutch, finding it difficult to feed the black population, responded by allotting plots of land to manqueron slaves, upon which the slaves were expected to grow their own crops. Since success necessarily depended upon adequate rainfall, a distinctive form of Tambú evolved to attend the situation—a practical application given Curaçao's poor soil conditions and frequent droughts. Performed by a single drum soloist, with neither *herú* nor accompanying text vocalization, *Yama Áwaseru òf lòs Nubia* featured rhythms and effects that replicated the sounds of a thunderstorm—thunder, lightning, and the gentle sounds of falling raindrops. Tambúreros added their own variations and stylistic effects to the sounds and rhythms of the storm, further encouraging the clouds to "loosen" and the needed rain to fall. Yama Áwaseru òf lòs Nubia became increasingly improvisational in nature, as drummers freely took rhythmic liberties, heightening the rhythms with ornamentation consisting of rhythmic slaps and additional beats.

A fifth Tambú type evolving during slavery was one expressly designed for the purpose of nourishing the soul of the *barí*. Called *Sanger pa Tambú* ("Blood for the Tambú"), it commenced when one or more participants called out the phrase *"Sounda di Tambú!"* ("Play the Tambú!"). Two men were expected to immediately leave the dance floor to fetch the long *kokomakaku* sticks. Adversaries would then square off much as in the conventional kokomakaku, although without the animosity. The moment blood was drawn, the stick fighting stopped. A measure of blood would be gathered and placed into a prepared hole in the dirt near the drum in order to nourish the instrument—it being believed the spirit of a Tambú drum required occasional blood nourishment to remain healthy and strong. As Rosalia reminds, "Our tradition teaches us that once in a while the Tambú needs to drink some blood" (1997: 75).

Although Dutch officials may have been willing to ignore Tambú at first, when anti-white sentiments began to grow among the manquerons, ordinances were quickly issued as a means of control. The ordinance titled *Regels tegen Schlecht Gedrag en voor de Betere Discipline van Zwarten en Mulattin* ("Rules against Bad Behavior and for the Better Discipline of Blacks and Mulattos"), instigated in 1740, was the first of many laws meant to limit Afro-Curaçaoan cultural activities. Tambú, cited as a particularly troublesome source of *schlecht gedrag* ("bad behavior"), became a specific target of the law. Authorities suggested such events promoted *rampzalige resultaten* ("disastrous results"), pointing to the kokomakaku stick fighting as one example. Those who dared question the *Regels* or who openly disobeyed them were subjected to imprisonment or worse, including being branded with hot irons or whipped with a *bulpres* (a stretched and dried bull's penis, wrapped with rope).

In 1741, the repression of *schlecht gedrag* was expanded as the *Verbod van Vergaderingen door Zwarte Mensen en Mulattin* ("Prohibition of Meetings by Black People and Mulattos") prohibited Afro-Curaçaoans from congregating in groups of seven or more. This proved particularly devastating to Tambú and other manqueron customs. With this rule, even funeral obsequies became highly restricted, with the particularly oppressive effect of depriving the Afro-community of the opportunity to pay final respects to the deceased. Without the proper funeral rites, families feared the souls of their loved ones were unable to reach Venezuela. The souls of loved ones would be left to spend eternity floundering aimlessly; or worse, they would forever haunt family members for neglecting them, bringing bad luck to bear upon the family and community.

Such government ordinances forced followers to practice Tambú in secret. Events moved underground, and the Tambú music, in response, transformed to accommodate its now clandestine setting. Considered too loud, the iron instruments were often abandoned, with foot stomps and hand claps becoming more prominent, sometimes providing the rhythms previously heard from the iron. In similar fashion, the drum, played previously with open palm, was now performed upon with a closed palm, which produced a quieter, more muffled sound. As may be surmised, clandestine Tambú performances also required secretive new methods of announcement. Rituals from then on were called together with a single muted slap by the drummer (called *yamada*). Because the yamada was sometimes too quiet to be easily heard, community members, in anticipation of a performance, were said to have placed their ears to the ground to listen for faint vibrations directing them to the location of such events.

While traditional Tambú was performed at the crossroad intersections of roads and pathways, government ordinances had the effect of moving performances to secret locations, called *hòfis*. Hidden in the shadows of shade trees, swept free of sticks and brush, hòfis were just large enough to accommodate a circle of musicians, dancers, and a few audience participants. Concerned that the Tambú drum sounds could be swept along with the island's strong western winds, blown toward the direction of the plantation houses, hòfis were usually set up at the easternmost corners of the estates, with the Tambú events themselves relegated to the late evenings (Juliana 1983, 1987). The essence of the crossroads was maintained in these secret Tambú through symbolic re-creations made by sprinkling libations at the four corners of an imagined square (Rosalia, personal communication, December 30, 2001). (A photo of a hòfi appears in fig. 3.1.)

While the hòfi emerged as one alternative performance space, devotees also began bringing the Tambú inside slave quarters for added privacy. These Tambú events assumed the title *Tambú di Kas* ("Tambú for Houses"), and were meant for even smaller performance venues. Because the slave quarters may have had wooden or cement floors, the sounds of the dancing, singing, and drumming tended to be amplified. In efforts to keep performances from being discovered, Tambú di Kas necessarily developed special performance techniques meant to minimize the sound level. The piercing clangor of herú (overpowering in small spaces) again was toned down, not only by limiting the number of instrumentalists, but also by replacing the iron instruments themselves with kitchen knives. Kitchen knives not only produced a softer tone, but had the added advantage of being both more readily accessible and easily hidden. In the same vein, tables and chairs also transformed into

Figure 3.1. A photo of the *hòfi* from Landhuis Santa Crus. Photo: Curaçao
Historical Archives.

semi-adequate drum replacements if a barí was unavailable. Smaller spaces
also meant that fewer Tambú followers could attend, and even fewer dancers
could participate. To ensure reasonably sized audiences, guests were invited
by word of mouth. This had the added effect of elevating Tambú to the status of a higher social function.

Tambú's continued evolution took it along increasingly secular lines, a
widening range of purpose that presented Tambú more as a process than as
an end in itself. One of Tambú's earliest secular functions was the dissemination of information. Tantamount to a local newspaper, these particular
Tambú would help circulate the island's latest gossip and community news.
With time, Tambú's news scope broadened to supplement local news with
newsworthy items from plantations and communities beyond Curaçao's
borders, including news from surrounding Caribbean islands, and eventually from as far abroad as South America and the Netherlands. Van Meeteran
notes how "news from other countries was welcome" to members of the
Afro-community (1947: 81). Tambú became increasingly sophisticated in
terms of its presentation, eventually supplementing news reports with a
public forum in which Afro-Curaçaoans could convey their personal psy-

chological reactions to the world, or editorialize on the social and political issues that affected them.

A second secular Tambú to emerge during the slave years was one meant to settle disputes. To the early Afro-Curaçaoans, words possessed power. This fact is clearly demonstrated in the Curaçaoan proverb: *"Palabra na sènter ta guera"* ("Words are at the center of war"). The dominant Dutch society allowed early Afro-Curaçaoans little recourse in the resolution of problems and differences between their own peers. The normal means to resolve such conflict was to challenge one's adversary to a war of words. Similar to Trinidad's *picong*, this form of Tambú offered enslaved blacks the opportunity to castigate anyone whose actions or views they deemed contrary to their own. As noted in chapter 1, someone wishing to punish a perceived backslider in this fashion could enlist the services of a well-respected Tambú singer to attack the malefactor in song. Because those so "attacked" were free to reciprocate in kind, virtual "Tambú battles" ensued. Audience reaction determined the winners and losers according to which antagonist had presented the most clever argument. In the end, a handshake would often indicate that differences had been resolved.

Historian Elis Juliana cites an interesting and humorous documented example: It seems the *Shon* ("slave proprietors") of two slave communities had come to some sort of dispute over an issue now forgotten. Their disagreement, however, caused one Shon Banban from the plantation Soledat to suffer physical attack at the hands of the other Shon. It seems Shon Banban, though physically larger, simply turned and walked away rather than fight. The event caused slaves of both plantations to challenge one another to Tambú battles over whose Shon was made to appear the more foolish by their actions. The ensuing battle of words was recorded for posterity in the following Tambú:

Shon Banban 'i Soledat	Shon Banban from Soledat,
Kón bo ke laga morto dalbu!	How can you let such a man hit you!

The slaves of the opposing Shon retaliated with their own Tambú, singing:

Morto kier, morto por	If there is a will, there is a way

In the end, this simple yet direct response emerged victorious (Juliana 1983: 19). Of course, not all Tambú battles were over marginal disagreements, nor did they always end so neatly. The hurling of invective could degenerate into the pushing and shoving game known as *trankamentu.* If disputants got too carried away, the dispute might even escalate into a kokomakaku, the battle with sticks.

As anti-white sentiments continued to grow, more strict rules against Tambú were instigated. In 1750, a few decades before the famous revolt, an ordinance was instituted that banned the singing of songs that were believed to accompany outlawed events like Tambú. For their part, the Dutch countered by censuring anyone seen carrying Tambú instruments, or dressing in outfits that might be construed as Tambú costuming. In 1766, *Verbod van het Lopen van de Straten mit een Kokomakaku* ("Prohibition of Walking the Streets with a Kokomakaku Stick") made it unlawful for any black individual to walk carrying a stick, and in 1780 the laws were expanded again with *Verbod van het Lopen van de Straten met een Barí* ("Prohibition of Walking the Streets with a Barí Drum"). Violators were deemed rebels who threatened "the overall tranquility of the public" (Rosalia 1997: 108).

Eventual legislation authorized officials to confiscate Tambú drums or to destroy them onsite during any Tambú performance, regardless of sacred or secular variety, punishing tambúreros and Tambú participants alike. Determined to continue their festivities, Tambú participants devised alternative drums, ones that were lighter and more portable, easily moved between secret locations, or quickly hidden in case of discovery. For a time, simple household items were transformed into barí drums, which included a table top or bench; even kerosene cans emerged as particular favorites upon which to drum out Tambú rhythms. Such pieces were easily disguised, and could be hidden among normal household furniture. Rarely suspected by authorities, these newly designated wooden idiophones enabled the continuation of Tambú events, including funerals. When traditional barí drums were used, women took to wearing large, full skirts, with the idea that during raids they could temporarily sit on the drums, using the extra material to hide the instruments.

Tambú drummers who continued to play on actual drums also devised a new trend of painting their drums in the red, white, and blue of the Dutch flag, hoping respect for the colors of the queen would hold the police at bay. It was hoped that at the very least, authorities would refrain from destroying the drums. Drums painted in this manner were called *nobel barrels* by the enslaved community, and according to Rosalia, the idea proved successful in at least limiting officials from damaging the instruments. "Police had respect for [those] drum[s]," he writes. Still, although destruction of the instrument was avoided, officials were still just as prone to confiscate the instruments (Rosalia 1997: 148).

Drums continued to be confiscated after emancipation, and Afro-Curaçaoans in the hope of saving their instruments from being destroyed kept on painting them in the colors of the Dutch flag. It is therefore small wonder that over the course of time the storage areas of many Curaçao police stations became quite overcrowded with the seized nobel barrels. Local folk historians inform that police officials, loathe to destroy the patriotically painted drums, found a novel way to make money: "They would sell [the drums]. They would take away your Tambú and then just sell it back to you" (Rafaela, quoted by Rosalia 1997: 146). This ironic practice, Rafaela continues, was both widespread and maintained well into the twentieth century. "Thomas and I would be playing Tambú at one place, and the police would come and take the drum away. A week later, if we wanted our Tambú back, we would buy it from the police station" (ibid.).

With Tambú so tightly integrated into the social life of black Curaçaoans it is little surprise that the news of emancipation (which came in 1863) spread across the island in Tambú verse. Rene Rosalia documents this dramatic example (1997: 89–90):

Libertat!	Liberty!
Libertat, gatlité	Gallant Liberty
Bo n' ta batimi ku chapara	You will not beat me with whip
Libertat, gatlité	Gallant Liberty
Ora Shon tin gan'i bati	When the slave owner feels moved to beat someone
Libertat, gatlité	Gallant Liberty
Shon bai bati Shon su mama	The slave owner can go beat his mother

A second example, documented by the priest Paul Brenneker, expresses the joy of freedom (1974):

Ban!	Let us Go!
Mi n' ta laba tayó	I will not wash the dishes
Awor ta djaka ta laba tayó	Let the rats wash the dishes now
Ban, Ban, Ban, Ban!	Let us go, Let us go, Let us go, Let us go!
Ban mira Shon su kara	Let us go behold slave owner's face
Awor ta pushinan lo kohe	Let the cats now catch rats now
raton pa Shon	catch rats for the slave owner
Awor katibu a kaba	Now there are no more slaves
N' tin katibu mas	No slaves anymore

While the jubilation and relief thus expressed may reveal the Afro-Curaçaoans' hope for a brighter future, the ensuing reality was far from ideal. Ex-slaves were allotted tiny plots in the island's most barren reaches, and most found themselves unable to survive solely on the land. Many resigned themselves to poorly paid positions on the very plantations they had recently so joyously left. Thus, while emancipation brought freedom in the legal sense, most Afro-Curaçaoans remained subordinate both socially and economically to their former proprietors (Römer 1981: 42).

Government repression of Montamentu and Tambú continued. In 1872, the ordinance *Naar de Raadsbesluit voor Vieren Toeschouwers Volgorde, Rustig, en Zekerheidstelling voort naar de Eiland van Curaçao* ("The Decree to Keep Public Order, Tranquility, and Security on the Island of Curaçao") was sanctioned. This law empowered white authorities to use physical force against any Afro-Curaçaoan perceived endangering the public order, tranquility, and security. While the letter of the law suggested anyone observing untoward behavior within the Afro-Curaçaoan community should summon the police, it was not mandatory they do so. In effect, the ordinance basically empowered vigilante whites to judge and punish blacks as they saw fit without fear of personal legal consequence. The decree further specified a list of punishable behavior that included dancing and jumping—both of which might be associated with the practice of Tambú.

In 1884, another harsh law (Rosalia 1997: 112), *Onherroepelijk van Standplaats Talen* ("Definition of Living Languages"), specified French, English, German, Spanish, and Dutch as *standplaats* ("living" and therefore

legal) languages. These languages were officially deemed "allowable" on Curaçao, while the creole language Papiamento was singled out as *stroomloos*
(dead, and therefore banned from being spoken in public places). The significance of language in defining community identity cannot be overstated.
"Language carries culture," writes Ngũgĩ wa Thiong'o. Language invokes
"the entire body of values by which we come to perceive ourselves and our
place in the world" (1997 [1981]: 290). Language provides "the terms by
which reality may be constituted [and] the names by which reality may be
'known'" (Ashcroft et al. 1995: 283). Restraint of language "annihilates a people's belief in their names," as well as "in their environment, in their heritage
of struggle, in their unity, in their capacities and ultimately in themselves"
(Ngũgĩ 1997 [1981]). As Rosalia emphasizes, after *Onherroepelijk van Standplaats Talen,* even simple greetings between passersby could no longer be exchanged in Papiamento. In response, Afro-Curaçaoans adopted the custom
of speaking through hand gestures and body movement—a phenomenon
that continues on Curaçao into the present day (Rosalia 1997: 112).

Throughout the nineteenth and twentieth centuries, the church, too,
voiced criticism toward Tambú. "Tambú is an invention of the devil," priests
regularly warned from the pulpit, offering frequent depictions of a demonic
character of African descent, often unclothed and playing a Tambú drum
(Juliana 1990: 4). As we have already seen, Tambú was often decried from
the pulpit. Those even merely suspected of participating in it were strong-
ly warned that their very place in heaven was in jeopardy (Juliana 1987,
1990). In addition to denouncing Tambú, priests were known to rail against
Montamentu as well, and were the first to instigate the epithet *Brua* in reference to its followers.

Not surprisingly, the practice of the religious Tambú declined in popularity during the nineteenth and twentieth centuries. However, instead of
turning away entirely, many Afro-Curaçaoans began participating in secular versions of Tambú, which, it was hoped, would be perceived in a more
socially acceptable light. Parties were quick to emerge, with non-religious
Tambú performed as entertainment. Generally occurring on weekends, "beginning on Friday nights and continuing, without stopping, until Sunday
night" (Rosalia 1997: 77), these party Tambú maintained the same musical
structure as their religious precedents. Following the familiar binary form,
the habrí section of the party Tambú still featured the solo singer, the accompanying single barí and several chapi maintaining the familiar Tambú

rhythmic patterns. Audience members at these performances remained quiet during the habrí, gently swaying side to side as they listened intently to the text, which rather than being organized around spiritual themes, took on the form of social commentary. Just as in religious Tambú, a wave of the singer's hand signaled the será section to commence. Thus, a call and response between the soloist and chorus began, with audiences now free to dance, which they did with hand clapping (*brassa*), and foot stomping (*pisotea*). While the two varieties of Tambú—religious and *parzee* (secular)—appeared similar on the outside, their purpose (and, therefore, textual content) maintained opposite spectrums. Since participants would congregate at secular Tambú parties for the main purpose of having a good time, few sought to attain trance states at secular events.

Most Tambú performed for socializing were staged in private homes. As a result, the term *Tambú di Kas*, which was first coined during slavery, was brought back into vogue. While *Tambú di Kas* was previously used in conjunction with the religious Tambú, today the term is associated nearly exclusively with the party Tambú. The phrase brings sly smiles to the faces of Afro-Curaçaoan people. According to a local musician and drummer, "*Tambú di Kas* means to have a good time!" (Randall, personal communication, August 13, 2000). Another musician adds, "*Tambú di Kas* is the name for partying!" He then clarifies that "It means dancing, card-playing, and lots of drinking!" (Eugene, personal communication, August 5, 1997).

Some private homes became popular during the nineteenth and early twentieth centuries as venues for infamous Tambú parties. Many remain recognized as such to the present day (especially those located in downtown Willemstad's Hanch'i Punda Street). Senior Curaçaoan native Aluisio Ocalia remembers one particularly raucous *Tambú di Kas* party he attended as a child in the early twentieth century. The celebration, he recalls (located in a house in the area *Fleur de Mari*), was a *Tambú dóbel* ("double Tambú"), with two Tambú events going on simultaneously—one in the living room, another in the backyard. Ocalia recalls how the *Tambú dóbel* went on for eight days, "*un padilanti un den adrei. E flu a sak bai abou!*" ("[until] the floor of [the] house broke with everyone on it. And [finally] we sat down!") (Ocalia, as quoted by Rosalia 1997: 77).

Another popular type of secular Tambú that emerged during the nineteenth century was one distinguished for its tendency to move from place to place. *Paranda di Tambú* ("Tambú Parade"), as it was called, became especially popular on New Year's Eve, and involved participants marching from house to house, or from neighborhood to neighborhood, to the rhythms of Tambú. The primary function of Paranda di Tambú was as part of *Manda Fuku Bai*. Through the performance of this Tambú, it was believed the harmful negativity accrued during the closing year could be driven out of each house along the way. Out of gratitude, home owners offered participants food and drink in hopes they would escort bad spirits out of their houses and neighborhoods, and leave them uncontaminated to face the new year. Passersby were free to join the parade, and each stopover brought new members to the procession. Tambú rhythms ostensibly purified the air as the assemblage went along, primarily on foot, sometimes transported aboard a *trúk di palu* (or "wooden pickup truck"). It was traditionally led by an Obeah-man or -woman, organized by people who presumably attribute a particularly difficult year due to the effects of visiting bad spirits. The Obeah-man or -woman would prescribe charms and herbal medicines to bring better fortune for the year ahead. Sometimes a *klabu-klabu* ("ritual cleansing bath") would be prescribed, requiring participants to jump into the sea at 12:00 midnight in belief the salt water will purify body and soul. Other situations might call for the Obeah leader to prescribe the *byla pa tira fuku afó* ("dance to get rid of bad spirits")—dancing and sweating to Tambú being an ostensibly effective countermeasure to fuku.

Another Tambú type popular during New Year's was *Bandera di Tambú* (or the "Tambú of the Little Flags"). It too enjoyed widespread recognition during the nineteenth and early twentieth centuries. Bandera di Tambú involved small flags or bits of colored paper (*bandera*), upon which were inscribed words and phrases to be used as themes for improvised Tambú songs. The Tambú singer (*pregon*) would gather the bandera and improvise lyrics, to the delight of audiences who stood quietly to hear the news and latest gossip. This was done in the habrí section of Bandera di Tambú, which was notorious for vulgarities and lies, gossip and ideas that most preferred to write down anonymously rather than express aloud. Texts were often scribed in metaphors, and most generally left the public questioning who might have written them, and for whom they might have been intended. The following será—a call and response—was essentially a dialogue between soloist and audience members, who danced and clapped hands until refocusing once again on the bandera lyrics.

Oftentimes, bandera were *sold* to the Afro-Curaçaoan public, with town businesses and street vendors hawking collections of colored papers and flags to anxious patrons, who pinned them to their clothing and hats, or tied them to trees and bushes in their front yards. Sometimes bandera were hung on people's fences, or even affixed to their front doors. Although Bandera di Tambú was often used as punishment for the perceived inappropriate behavior of members of the immediate community, it could just as easily and effectively ridicule misuse of governmental or religious power. "The Dutch government has their penalties, and we have ours," one Curaçaoan explained to the author. "When you've served your time in prison, you can leave. If you have a Tambú written about you, you're sanctioned for life! A Tambú will stay around forever!" (Pincho, personal communication, December 29, 2001). Another individual described how Bandera di Tambú can degenerate into "all-out war!" As he explained to the author, "If your enemy writes a bandera against you, you may hire a Tambú singer to write and sing an even worse bandera against the enemy" (Reymound, personal communication, November 20, 2000).

Described as a "graceful use of data" by historian Johannes Hartog (1961: 888), the Bandera di Tambú found fair game in any matter identified as needing improvement—as the following lyrics suggest (Juliana 1987: 61).

Ai kabaraon ta mi nómber	Shrimp is the name,
Mi bibá ta bou'i lodo.	Life in the mud is my game.
Si bo mirami riba tera	If you see me above the ground
Ta ko'i reda lo mi tin!	Then it is gossip that I bring!

Messages expressed via Bandera di Tambú could be as decadent as they could be harsh. Two examples, both from the early twentieth century, follow (Rosalia 1997: 80–85):

Directed to a woman perceived as vain:

> "*Dushi, pa tantu wapu ku bo ta. Bo por laga sapu pishi den bo kara?*"

> ("Honey, as beautiful as you may be, how can you allow a frog to piss in your face?")

Directed to the "other woman" in efforts to expose a man's infidelity:

> "*Bo kucara den bo wea ki mishié den mi tayó?*"

> ("The spoon in your pot, what is it doing in my dish?")

With Tambú's metamorphosis from sacred ritual to popular social event, the growing tendency in the late nineteenth and twentieth centuries was for pregon lead singers to offer their art as a platform for satire and other social commentary challenging elitist white values and institutions. Spirited pregons sometimes went so far as to improvise texts suggesting guidelines for action—offering possible ways to correct the perceived social injustices and unfair social conditions of which they sang. More cautious singers might mask such satirical counter-narratives through the use of code words understandable only to social insiders. Often this type of criticism and satirical reference went unnoticed by governmental and church officials—the two most popular targets of all Tambú criticism. Afro-Curaçaoans thus felt ownership over the satirical Tambú, fueling cultural empowerment.

A particularly fascinating example of Tambú satire directed toward the Catholic Church is represented in the following Tambú passage (Rosalia 1997: 92). The text focuses on how church officials, quick to impose set rules for their constituents, do not necessarily hold themselves accountable to the same restrictions. This Tambú recounts the story of a nun who ignored her vows of celibacy and became pregnant. It utilizes the camouflaged title word, *Kongrenis* (Papiamento for a female member of the church).

Kongrenis	Kongrenis
Ta un kachó mi tabatin	It is a dog that I had
Tende kon m'a yam'é	Listen to how I named him
M'a mara un sinta na su garganta	I put a band around his neck,
Dun'ele nòmber di Kongrenis	And gave him the name *Kongrenis*

Political figures also supplied Tambú with plenty of apt subject matter. Curaçao's infamous Governor Rouville (1866–1870), who was particularly disliked by Afro-Curaçaoans for his ambivalence toward civil rights, is lampooned in the following Tambú, titled *Mener Rouville* (Brenneker 1974):

Mener Rouville	Governor Rouville
Mener Rouville a bin Kórsou	The Governor Rouvill came to Curaçao

El a hasi tempu ta skarsedat	But he came only briefly
Kos ku el a hasi bon	The only good thing that he did
K'el a pone luza na kaya skur	Was to put some lights in the dark streets
Uniko kos ku el a hasi bon	The only good thing that he did
K'el a pone lampi na kayanan	Was to put some lights in the dark street

It is easy to understand that satire and invective set forth in these secular Tambú performances would stir considerable prickly concern among state and church officials, who protested the bawdy and raucous nature of such events. Again in an effort to limit their performance, authorities stepped up attacks against the secular Tambú, denouncing it as liable to provoke riots and violence, and reiterating opinions that the secular Tambú equaled the sacred Tambú in its projection of low-class behavior.

Church administrators became just as adamant as state officials in their efforts to combat the secular Tambú. Aware that the police had been totally unable to stamp out Tambú through threats and the confiscation of drums, the church tackled the problem from a different position. The subject of dance became the main target of the church, and officials and priests now complained that it was the Tambú dance moves that specifically embodied evil. The pulpit became the soapbox for public condemnation of dancing as "solely a sexual act between man and woman" (Rosalia 1997: 69). Tambú, they claimed, involved "movements that are not Christian" (Juliana 1990: 3). Since both the sacred and secular Tambú made use of exactly the same dance movements, both forms of Tambú came under attack. In one blistering sermon, Monsieur Niewindt protested, "You can hear in the streets and in the town the noises of Tambú drummers and this so-called singing, or better said, screaming, by these shameless black women [who] . . . take turns doing this appalling dance." Niewindt went on to pronounce, "This has prompted [Dutch] Protestants to feel ashamed, and . . . say that Curaçao is becoming more like Africa—an uncivilized place" (Niewindt, quoted by Brusse 1969: 93).

The church's disdain for Tambú became directed specifically to the dancing involved, as evidenced by its liberal sprinkling of the epithet *Byla di pelvis* ("Dance of the pelvis") in sermons and commentaries. When it became evident such rhetoric was having little effect, participation in either the religious or secular Tambú became deemed reason enough for excommunication—a threat that continues to gravely curtail the participation in Tambú among more pious Afro-Curaçaoans even into the twenty-first century. As participation in Tambú began to dwindle, the situation was reflected in Afro-Curaçaoan vernacular with phrases like *Tambú di lamentu* ("Tambú of grief") being replaced by *Tambú di sanka* ("Tambú of the behind"), and *Brua* used in place of Montamentu (with many Afro-Curaçaoans today unaware that Montamentu was the initial title of the religion).

Cultural discrimination continued to be legislated on Curaçao in the twentieth century, with the focus now on dance. In 1935, *Verbod van Tambú Zonder Geëigend Vergunnig* ("Prohibition of Tambú without Proper Permits") directed would-be Tambú organizers first to propose their ideas to Curaçao's chief of police. Requests were often denied, on the basis of inadequate parking, too many invited guests, or inappropriateness of location. All decisions faced a standard waiting period of around two months. The ordinance furthermore designated that two or more people from separate residences could not dance with each other without the proper permit, and in petitioning for a Tambú gathering, organizers needed to sign papers to the effect that no dancing would take place. In addition, they needed to specify exact dates, a list of what music would be specifically played, and present a guest list naming everyone who would attend. Needless to say, this ordinance (still in effect to the present day) eliminated the possibility for spontaneous Tambú gatherings, and the consequences of singling out dancing for regulation severely crippled Tambú's continuation as a vehicle for memory. Without dance, Tambú was compelled to become a spectator event rather than one to be participated in. Without participation, events were removed from their meaningful historical and cultural context, unable to fulfill their original promise of unification and strength. With Curaçaoan police far more likely to seek out Tambú infractions in urban than rural areas, Tambú party hosts denied proper permits increasingly turned to the island's outskirts to hold clandestine parties. As a result, Tambú gradually assumed a rural connotation. Even today, most Tambú parties tend to be carried out in the Bandabao and Bandariba communities (the two farthest points of the island).

The decades of the 1960s and '70s dawned upon an era of great political unrest. Shell Oil revenues were skyrocketing—matched only by a corresponding growth in governmental bureaucracy and authority. While a number of lucrative government jobs were created, these evolving positions were filled again and again by Dutch-born individuals—much to the discouragement of both Afro-Curaçaoans and their local white counterparts. Shell constructed special insular communities for these Dutch employees and their families in the neighborhoods, which had their own superior schools, soccer fields, supermarkets, restaurants, and movie theaters. The newly arrived Holland Dutch soon emerged as a powerful symbol to both emulate and resent (Rupert 1999).

Ironically, a shared discontent among Curaçao's white and black populations served to unite the two formerly disparate groups, and on May 30, 1969, they joined forces in a politically charged riot known today as "The May Movement," which resulted in loss of life and millions of dollars in property damage. Although the May Movement may have resulted in only minor changes in the island's political system, it did have the effect of bridging divisions between white Curaçaoans and black Curaçaoans in favor of the more inclusive term *Antillean*. Papiamento became regarded as the language of choice soon after the May Movement, precisely because it separated Antilleans (white and black) from the Dutch. In further attempts to differentiate, Antilleans sought musical art forms indigenous to Curaçao. Heading the way was the *tumba*, a local music and dance genre that, free of religious association, was integrated into local carnival proceedings and highlighted at a specially created festival appropriately titled *Tumba Festival*. A few years later, a circle of Afro-Curaçaoan scholars, many armed with graduate degrees earned in the Netherlands, returned to their home island committed to establishing a more African-centered sensibility among the Afro-Curaçaoan people. Among their goals was to get the Curaçaoan government to reconsider its restrictions against Tambú. Although no one took immediate notice of these activists, their continued efforts sparked a revolution of thought. These self-proclaimed Afro-culturalists eventually garnered enough of a following that, by degrees, both the Curaçaoan government and the Catholic Church were compelled to appease their demands, tolerating folkloric Tambú performances on the grounds of their historical significance, and temporarily relaxing rigid ordinances during certain months of the year—namely November, December, and January. Since Tambú activity was legally sanctioned during these allotted months, the period has become known as Tambú Season. Yet today, two separate permits are required of hosts holding Tambú gatherings, even during Tambú Season. One permit is required for the event itself; and a second is needed if the host wants to have dancing at the event.

Presently, radio stations are allowed to legally air Tambú recordings during Tambú Season (provided only non-political and non-religious Tambú be played and, even then, no more than two Tambú pieces consecutively). "We are given a list of Tambú recordings that we are allowed to play," explains one radio DJ. "We are not told specifically that we can or cannot play a certain Tambú song, but I think this list speaks for itself" (Singh, personal communication, January 5, 2002). Each year Tambú bands form with the purpose of recording hit songs for the upcoming Tambú Season. Since radio play represents the primary factor in how popular their music ultimately proves, most current Tambú bands decide to toe the line in writing texts conforming to acceptable themes of love and betrayal.

Roy Wagner categorizes the world's greatest inventions as those which undergo constant reinvention—ones that evolve "many times . . . as [they are] taught, learned, used, and improved, often in combination with other inventions" (1986: 10). Tambú's versatility of social function has endowed Afro-Curaçaoans with a repository for cultural memory, a vehicle of social criticism, an icon of religious ritual, and a means of social regeneration. "Like everything which is historical," Tambú, to borrow the words of Stuart Hall, is "far from . . . externally fixed in some essentialized past" (1989: 70). It is "always relevant to its social context" (Finkelstein 2000: 235), always responding to "the continuous 'play' of history, culture and power" (Hall 1989: 70). The Afro-Curaçaoan community, like Tambú itself, has evolved with the changing times.

Tambú encodes aural practices in culturally meaningful ways, constituting not only communication but also, over time, recollection and commemoration. Tambú may present guidelines for action, or suggest ways to correct perceived unjust social conditions. It may represent a collective action, or challenge accepted power relationships, following what Anthony Giddens calls "life politics," or one that concerns "issues . . . of self-actualization in post-traditional contexts" (1991: 214). Tambú also fulfills the purpose of retelling history from an Afro-Curaçaoan perspective, empowering succeeding generations with a culturally perceived past in accordance to specific needs within the present. In this way, Tambú reconfigures the past, endowing history with meaning and continuity, projecting a sense of what the future may hold. Borrowing upon the words of Hayden White, Tambú represents a "kind of allegory" within whose heart beats the "latent or manifest purpose" of "moraliz[ing] the events . . . which it treats" (1981: 13–14).

In Tambú, where a variety of genres exist, from the sacred to the secular, audiences have developed different views regarding its performance. This ability to persuade listeners in different ways lies again with Tambú's unique structure. Just as the habrí and será sections enable many different deities to arrive at a religious Tambú, so too do the habrí and será facilitate a variety of interpretations. Listeners step into the story the Tambú singer presents. Those who agree with the text's point of view re-create, through dance, the world projected in the song; those who disagree, however, are still invited to at least consider the alternative through similar interactive involvement with the singer and the attending musicians. Interpretive communities form around Tambú songs, strengthening collective identity and providing a basis upon which social relationships may be forged. In this way, Tambú's edifying strength lies beyond the textual words and more in its ability to stimulate empathy and order through active communication, and unite Tambú singers, musicians, and audience members into an effective "we."

As Wolfgang Iser writes, "Text only takes on life when it is realized" (1972: 279). The effectiveness of Tambú lies with the audience's ability and willingness to make the necessary connections between presentation and intention (Leitch 1986: 63). The active listener "sets the work in motion," and is ultimately edified "in the awakening of responses within himself" (Iser 1972: 280). Connections, when they succeed, "are the product of the reader/listener's mind and not simply a perception of what is written or heard" (Davis 2002: 16). Borrowing this analysis, Tambú projects a "virtual dimension of the text" by which the message stirs an audience's response. This virtual dimension exists as "the coming together of text and imagination" (Iser 1972: 284).

As a social process, Tambú song also requires the participation of two parties: the singer (text) and an interpretive audience (imagination). Tambú's structural form is also comprised of two parts: the habrí and the será (with the occasional introduction). The first part, the habrí, emphasizes the text; audience members are expected to assume the role of active listeners, contemplating and evaluating the song text. During the habrí, the solo singer (accompanied by the chapi iron instruments) conveys the textual message, capturing the audience with the song's story.

The Tambú singer is not only reporting a story, he or she is also inviting listeners to join in reflection, to assess and react to that story. Using the "speech acts" analysis of Mary Louise Pratt, taken from John L. Austin's original theory, the role of the Tambú singer is to produce in his hearers not only belief but also an imaginative and affective involvement in the state of affairs he is representing and an evaluative stance toward it. He intends them to share his wonder, amusement, terror, or admiration of the event. Ultimately, it would seem, what he is after is an interpretation of the problematic event, an assignment of meaning and value supported by the consensus of himself and his hearers. (1997: 136)

During the será, the focus is on group participation. Here audience members are invited to join in through hand claps, choral response, and the dance. Just prior to the será, audience members begin to slowly move in response to the rhythm, their hips and arms (referred to as *nan ta koncha*) adding kinetic force to the music. Dance, of course, represents a very special and traditional link between modern Afro-Curaçaoans and the memory of time-honored African culture. The dance, intricately woven into each Tambú performance, mobilizes a perceived ancestral history, and emerges as a locus of struggle, helping to reveal and represent an Afro-Curaçaoan cultural identity. Similarly, the clapping together of hands enables audience members to become part of the Tambú performance. By assuming the role of timekeeper, hand clappers free the chapi musicians to embellish the performance with improvisation and greater polyrhythmic texture. Similarly, through choral response, Tambú's communal aspect is stressed as audience members respond vocally to a textual message. During the será, audience members, when transformed into participants, serve Tambú's social function by "focusing attention [and] encouraging social solidarity" (Locke 1996: 74). Main ideas are offered by the solo singer, then repeated in unison and reinforced by choir and audience members. As such, a two-part idea is presented, with listeners' participation strengthening their overall understanding of the primary message.

In the spirit of the words of Paul Carter, who writes, "For by the act of place-naming, space is transformed symbolically into a place, that is, a space with a history" (1987: xxiv), Tambú represents more than a mere "record" of the past. Possessed of numerous contrasting functions, Tambú confers meaning upon the past, and evolves with the evolving needs—or fears—of a community. Succeeding generations have continued to rediscover Tambú, refitting it again and again to changing contexts. More than simply a window into Afro-Caribbean roots, however, a study of Tambú uncovers what Stuart Hall insinuates as "Afro-Caribbean *routes*" (emphasis mine)—the points where Afro-Curaçaoans have transcended African antecedents to establish new and diverse definitions of self (1996).

◊ ◊ ◊ ◊ ◊

The Tambú singer waves his hand, commanding the start of the será. The rhythms of the chapi intensify as the audience gathers at the dance floor. With hands outstretched and hips swinging, we are given the opportunity to participate in the song we have just heard—to voice personal opinions, to evaluate or comment on the story, or to recount our own experiences. Tambú invites participation, and, through it, enables Afro-Curaçaoans to continue to transform their island homeland into a special place that is "a space with a history" (Carter 1987: xxiv).

Come join in the Tambú—part 2 is about to commence.

PART 2.

Será: Get Ready! Get Ready!
Poné Bo Kla! Poné Bo Kla!

Prepare for the Arrival of Our Ancestors
Prepará Bo pa e Jegada di Nos Antepasados

To remember is to place a part of the past in the service of conceptions and needs of the present. —BARRY SCHWARTZ

Yamada: The Call

Tambú, as we have seen, was born of the union between local meanings and elements acquired through "global flows"—the movement and interaction of culture. Tambú has continued to evolve via unique conjunctions of social, political, economic, and cultural change, with the religious Tambú emerging particularly remarkable in its ability to transform. Differences are not just tolerated in the religious Tambú; they are embraced and affirmed. Since its inception, it has recognized the cultural multiplicity in Curaçaoan society, and expressed the positive acknowledgment of that plurality. The binary structure of Tambú has been one key to its appeal: the *habrí,* offering an open-ended invitation, and the *será,* offering open communication with an appealing variety of deities. Its "open door" policy enables participants nearly limitless access to the supernatural.

While slavery may have provided Tambú with its initial influences, the twentieth century, marked by the entrance of many migrant workers relocating to Curaçao to work at Shell Oil, served to transform the religious

Tambú into one of the most diverse creole forms in the Caribbean. When Chinese immigrants arrived, they brought their statues of the Buddha, placing them on display in their homes and at the many stores and restaurants they established. The Buddha did not go unnoticed by the Afro-Curaçaoans. Those involved in Tambú accepted the Buddha into Tambú's growing pantheon of deities, summoning the Buddha specifically for purposes of acquiring fortune and good health, setting his statue on adoration tables alongside the lithographs of St. Anthony and sculptures of St. Barbara.

Curaçao's Indian community introduced to the island the incarnations of Lord Vishnu, a deity recognized for his acute ability to preserve the world by incarnating himself in different forms at times of crisis. Members from the island's Indian community placed pictures of Vishnu, and his incarnations, on the walls of their homes and business establishments, and organized them atop private and public altars adorned with flowers and candy pieces. In the transformative spirit of Tambú, Vishnu, too, was adopted by Afro-Curaçaoans, his pictures added to the Tambú altar.

Perhaps the largest number of migrants arrived from Surinam (Dutch Guiana). As members of an existing Dutch colony, Surinamese workers had the advantage of already being able to write and speak in Dutch, and as a result were generally allotted higher-paid managerial positions at Shell. Many arrived indoctrinated in the religious philosophies of *Winti*, an Afro-syncretized religion distinct to Surinam. Although Winti, a religion that remained separate from Catholicism during slave years, contains few ideological ties to Tambú, it has emerged as an important influence in modern Tambú. Not only has Tambú absorbed some of the lesser gods from Winti, many of Curaçao's current Tambú spiritual leaders are from Surinam, where they are recognized as powerful *bonu-men* (Winti priests).

The recent technological developments in communication earmarking the late twentieth and early twenty-first centuries—including media (from telephone to e-mail) and the dissemination of information (from the island's television cable system, called the Black Box, to the internet)—have come to represent Curaçao's newest wave of "global flows." Since Tambú has always been a symbiotic process, it seems reasonable that it would also adapt to the twenty-first century by integrating the spirits generated by globalization. The late president John F. Kennedy presents one recent example of a spirit invoked at current Tambú gatherings. His particular powers have been sought out during Tambú celebrations directed toward strengthening world peace and diplomacy. Even the spirit of Marilyn Monroe was summoned to attend one recent ritual, brought into Tambú as a colleague of Kennedy. As seems apparent, globalization need not so much diminish Tambú's role in the community, as reveal a strategy for survival that has been part of its history since the days of slavery. By virtue of its characteristic pluralism and continually evolving synthesis, Tambú represents a religion still developing—still growing.

Admittedly, conjuring up the spirits of African ancestors and Arawak Amerindians, and even Marilyn Monroe and JFK, piques the imagination. Revealed by this, though, is a willingness to embrace diversity—which goes to the core ideology of Afro-Curaçaoan culture. The remarkable ability of *each* soul to transcend death, to hold sway over the affairs of the still-living, presents a remarkably inclusive proclivity—even more remarkable in light of a pantheon comprising the spirits of the recently deceased as easily as those of ancient gods and mythological characters. While the powers of each individual deity vary greatly, from weak to strong, from general to specific, their collective organism provides an intermediary between the human and supernatural realms. Death is revealed, therefore, as a transformation, "a portal to the sacred world beyond, where productive and morally upright individuals, perceived by devotees to be powerful ancestral figures, can exercise significant influence on their progeny" (Desmangles 1992: 3). Religious Tambú's communion with the supernatural also reflects a solemn regard for all deceased elders, perceived as approachable (in the same sense as the revered gods themselves). From this perspective, the supernatural is given reality, and a matter of travel and exchange exists between Tambú followers, living and deceased. Thus, Tambú meets the spiritual needs of its devotees, and enables unlimited possibilities regarding communion with the spiritual realm.

Spiritual possession enables devotees to assume the identities of the deities, projecting the particular characteristics and mannerisms of these spirits to those attending the events, exercising the extraordinary powers and abilities ascribed the particular spiritual being. Under spiritual possession, "devotees . . . become mediums of their gods" (Raboteau 1978: 10–11), or put another way, they become what Sheila Walker pointedly calls "living gods" (Walker 1972: 166). While possession may be the most frequent medium through which spirit emissaries arrive at Tambú rituals, deities may also visit Tambú followers in dreams, where they relay messages and guidance. It is also believed that spirits can physically manifest themselves at rituals: one Tambú participant, for example, recalls seeing Marilyn Monroe physically "standing in a far corner. Although it was dark, I know it was her. She looked just like she does in her movies" (Irceline, personal communication, November 3, 1995). Tambú's emergence may have been a matter of holding on to a remembered Africanness, yet its durability in the New World seems the result of its acceptance and incorporation of so much diversity. Its continual inclusion of new deities represents the religion's constant ability and desire to evolve with the spiritual powers and influences that surround it, revealing a persistent and purposeful reinterpretation on the part of "its participants interpreting meaningfully what is happening around them, and 'making sense' of the world" (Hall 1997: 2). With one eye toward the past, and the other on the future, the religious Tambú continues to offer a satisfying (though open-ended) conclusion.

Despite Tambú's acceptance of the diversity it encounters, the religious Tambú itself continues to be misunderstood by many of the very people to whom it should hold the greatest meaningfulness. It has been called everything from fetishism and witchcraft to psychopathic—even criminal—behavior. Small wonder, then, that true followers feel compelled to cloak their involvement in secrecy. Yet, this is a secrecy that has been cultivated over many years. Religious Tambú events are announced today strictly by word of mouth, and participants tend publicly to disavow their involvement. Typical uninformed outsiders may spend many months on Curaçao before becoming aware that the sacred Tambú sustains any existence outside of an occasional historical presentation. My own first months on Curaçao were spent naïvely perplexed at the difficulty I encountered in getting the research for this book off the ground. Initial inquiries among locals evoked reactions ranging from surprised reticence to anger, with most conveying an unambiguous uncomfortability. Those willing to talk at all limited their dialogue to popular or seasonal Tambú. Most made it decidedly clear that anything relating to sacred Tambú was off-limits to discussion. One soon understands that while religious Tambú may continue in modern Afro-Curaçao, it is seldom acknowledged. Another surprising revelation was how very much misinterpreted Tambú is by most Curaçaoans—emblematic perhaps of the island's double-standard value system that began during the colonial years, and the ghost of which yet remains.

A middle-aged Afro-Curaçaoan woman I spoke with explained it this way: "Even though I don't believe in Tambú, I take no chances" (Zita, personal communication, September 14, 1995). In typical fashion, she still pays homage to Tambú customs, hanging straw brooms outside the back door "to sweep away the bad luck before it enters the house," and bathing with sea salts taken from specific locations "to keep our spirits clean" (ibid.). A local Curaçaoan businessman presents another conundrum. This individual, who purports not to believe in the powers of Tambú, makes regular visits to Santo Domingo to receive what he calls "discreet advice" from *Santería* leaders. The businessman is quick to explain that while he "do[es] not believe in Tambú . . . I make enemies in my work. And they might believe in Tambú. I cannot be too careful" (Vernon, personal communication, August 8, 1997). Like many, this man feels none of the ignominy attached to Tambú when attending Santería. While Tambú is denounced for its association with Africa, Santería, a syncretized religion with similar African origins, is admired for its connection to Roman Catholicism. To this way of thinking, Tambú remains closely aligned with Africa (therefore ostensibly vulgar and second-class), while Santería and similar religions, including Vodou, have somehow managed to transcend such associations. A common practice has emerged on Curaçao, with Afro-Curaçaoans often traveling outside the island to visit with spiritual leaders from other Afro-syncretized societies, like those residing in the Dominican Republic and Colombia; yet, they remain quick to denounce acceptance of Tambú.

That Afro-Curaçaoans should regard Santería differently than they do Tambú reveals a remarkable irony. Both of these religions project similar objectives, and both reflect a similar history of origin, yet Tambú is held as offensive while Santería is not. Particular irony lies in the observation that many who disparage Tambú continue to hold to some of its customs—the hanging of straw brooms and the bathing in sea salts are two prime examples. If my research taught me anything, it is that a great discrepancy exists. The religious Tambú exists at the intersection of numerous cultural processes—at the crossroads of social and individual experience, somewhere between the cultural Self and the "Other."

From early on, the Othering of Afro-Curaçaoans amounted to cultural repression, provoked by governmental and church officials. Today, the situation still exists, yet now it involves participation by the Afro-Curaçaoans, with the religious Tambú emerging as the primary measure by which to distinguish the Self from the Other. With the process of Othering coming now full circle, many Afro-Curaçaoans have begun to view themselves "through the distorting focus of borrowed glasses" (Ngũgĩ 1997 [1981]: 90), and to blindly accept a distorted "image of self . . . identical with the European image of Africa" (ibid.: 30), to use the words of Kenyan writer Ngũgĩ wa Thiong'o. Because the officially accepted ideas about the religious Tambú (and the Afro-Curaçaoans who associate with it) have been manipulated in ways to suit the Curaçaoan dominant society, it has fallen victim to a misuse of power, which does nothing to salve the distorted self-definitions already held by Afro-Curaçaoans who "buy in" to the sanctioned design. Such exploitation braces up existing racial stereotypes: "not to reflect or represent a reality but to function as a disguise or mystification, of objective social relations" (Carby 1987: 22). In response, stereotypes surrounding the religious Tambú are further perpetuated, and call into question the very foundation of what currently passes as set legitimacy. Curaçao's current social shortcomings reinforce declining Afro-identity constructs and often protract the quagmire of white domination to become a vicious circle. As Sander Gilman reminds, "Because there is no real line between Self and the Other, an imaginary line must be drawn; and so that the illusion of an absolute difference between Self and Other is never troubled, this line is as dynamic in its ability to alter itself as is the Self" (1985: 18). When the Dutch and Catholic Church branded Tambú participants evil and low-class, the religious Tambú became the "imaginary line" Gilman describes.

Afirmashon: The Response

I am waiting outside a local bar near my apartment, fanning away the Curaçao evening heat, scanning the street for Rene Rosalia, who has agreed to escort me to my first Tambú ritual. Waiting for Rosalia, my thoughts wander: on one hand I eagerly anticipate finally becoming a part of Tambú; on the other, I'm apprehensive—reflecting upon the cryptic warnings received from well-intentioned Curaçaoan friends who advised against my participation. "Tambú is very bad!" forewarned one friend. "If you go, something very bad will happen to you" (Zita, personal communication, September 14, 1995). "You will never be the same again," another cautioned, adding, "there is only one true God, and He will punish you if you even step foot into Tambú!" (Maris, personal communication, September 14, 1995).

My reverie is interrupted by the arrival of Rosalia's dark-blue Toyota, and my fears evaporate as I slip in beside him for the thirty-minute drive to Bandabou on the westernmost tip of the island—quite a distance by Curaçao standards. Along the way, we discuss Tambú, and Rosalia offers much insight into the local culture, repeatedly voicing his concern that issues of identity and self-esteem lie at the heart of Afro-Curaçaoans' current problems, and that these issues had reached "crisis proportions." He illustrates his claim by explaining the colloquial use of the term *Loango*. The word specifically denotes people whose roots stem from Angola—the African nation from which the majority of Afro-Curaçaoan slaves were taken. Rosalia's voice rises as he explains that modern use of the word *Loango* is strictly an expression of insult: "A fighting word among young Curaçaoans"; a disparaging label used to designate people who culturally align themselves with things African. Considered an even more degrading insult is *Preto Loango*— translated as Black African. "It is like saying something bad about [your enemy's] mother," Rosalia explains. "You'd better be prepared to battle."

The service we plan to attend is being led by one of the most popular *Obeah-men* on Curaçao. At sixty years of age, with long experience, this respected leader is furthermore recognized as one of Curaçao's greatest Tambú singers. The date is September 29—a day assigned for the celebration of St. Miguel, the revered protector and guardian whom Afro-Curaçaoan followers tend to associate with the specific African deities *Ellegba* and *Ogun*.

We pull to a curb, stop. We seem to be in the middle of nowhere—our car the only one parked on this quiet neighborhood street: no lights denoting any sort of gathering, no indication of a Tambú ritual. Noting my wonder, Rosalia quietly reminds, "These events are secret. People park in ways not to bring attention to the event." After a walk around the block, we approach a large house which, I am to learn, is where the Obeah-man's ninety-five-year-old mother lives. We continue our walk in silence and darkness, making our way along a makeshift path to the back of the house. From there, a faint light in the distance draws us toward the muffled beating of a drum and, eventually, the hushed sounds of people talking. Finally, we reach a second, smaller house: a two-flat with an outdoor staircase jutting from the right. In front, carefully hidden behind tall bushes, a large garden lies framed with benches and several chairs, a stone path leading to the front door of the house. Within the garden, near the front door, a shrine constructed of stones, iron implements, and animal horns represents the entrance toward a person's spiritual path, shielding the home from unwelcome intruders and negative energy.

Inside the house are two rooms, the first of which holds several tables, each decorated by the Obeah-man earlier that day. Since this particular Tambú is for the celebration of St. Miguel, offerings represent the saint's

Figure 4.1. Photograph of an altar for St. Miguel (St. Michael) (main adoration table).
PHOTO BY AUTHOR.

preferred colors, his favorite foods and drinks. Tables-turned-altars are
adorned with red and green balloons, dishes of hard candies, bottles of rum
and whiskey, numerous vases of red roses, and a variety of candles—many
set atop empty wine bottles. Set upon the table, as well as hung upon nearby
walls, are lithographs depicting St. Miguel as Catholic Archangel: a mighty
warrior, armed with a sword and shield, battling a fierce dragon. Hovering
around the tables is a woman dressed all in white. She had been appointed
by the Obeah-man to watch over the adoration tables. In a corner sits the
Tambú drummer, and leaning toward him are two men beating the hand-
held *chapi* instruments. The sound of the iron is so loud and piercing, I
wonder why it had not been audible from the pathway.

In the second room, situated in back, stands another table. This one
is designed not as a shrine exclusively for St. Miguel, but rather as one in
acknowledgment of all deities and spiritual ancestors. Arranged atop it are
numerous pictures and statues of various Catholic saints, many depicted
as African descendants. As I continue scanning the table, I notice a Wayang
shadow puppet denoting the Indonesian epic hero Arjuna (the famous Pan-
dawa warrior), dressed here in plush purple, his head and tiara painted in

gold highlights. The puppet's arrival to Curaçao came via Surinam, a country that acquired its strong Indonesian influence soon after emancipation: both Surinam and Indonesia were occupied by the Netherlands—Surinam, as part of the Dutch West Indies, and Indonesia, as part of the Dutch East Indies—and, with the abolishment of slavery, Holland persuaded Indonesians to migrate to Surinam as indentured servants. Arjuna's presence in this ritual speaks volumes, not only about the diversity of Curaçao's cultural history, but how that diversity has been so brilliantly absorbed into Tambú—in this case, integrating African and Indonesian factors by way of Surinam.

To the left of the main adoration table, a rocking chair is placed to seat the Obeah-man during the ritual. As Rosalia motions for us to leave the house, the Obeah-man suddenly appears to express his personal hopes that I might find my first Tambú "a positive experience." Encouraging me to take pictures before the ritual, and to take notes during the event, he also invites me to contact him later in the week for a more in-depth interview. Somehow I find myself put at ease—surprised somehow that the leader is so accom-

Figure 4.2. Photograph of an altar for St. Miguel (St. Michael) (side adoration table).
PHOTO BY AUTHOR.

modating, so proud to offer guidance and explanation. Extending his re-gards to both Rosalia and to me, the Obeah-man leaves us as suddenly as he has appeared, and returns to his seclusion. The task of summoning a deity or ancestor is always done in private, Rosalia explains. As part of the sum-moning process, the Obeah-man must remain in seclusion. While alone, the Obeah-man also normally constructs a *Veve* on the ground floor, directly behind the house, drawn with corn meal or white flour. The Veve drawing is meant as a representation of the summoned saint, and functions during Tambú to usher in that saint.

Rosalia and I leave the house to return to the front garden, where we assume a pair of available seats. Looking around now I become suddenly aware that many more people have arrived, and that most are now standing and sitting around the garden area. Where did they all come from? How did this "secret" Tambú event manage to attract so many people? Most appear very comfortable and relaxed—a stark contrast to the considerable trepida-tion that now welled up again in my own mind. My eyes are drawn to the woman directly in front of me; her legs are crossed as she reads the daily newspaper. Sitting there so nonchalant, the woman appears more to be wait-ing for a bus than preparing to participate in a secretive ritual. Two other women stand near the shrine. They laugh as they discuss recent events at work. I have arrived at my first ritual so unsure about what to expect, and now it is the seeming normalcy and commonplaceness that I find most sur-prising—puzzling, really.

The time is nearing 8:00 PM—the time when the ritual is scheduled to commence. Although 8:00 had been the official start time given, most par-ticipants do not arrive until 9:00—or even shortly thereafter. The pungent smell of cigar smoke signals the arrival of the Obeah-man—and I recall hearing that only when spiritual possession is imminent will the Obeah-man light a cigar. The woman tending the adoration tables now walks as-sertively into the garden, and announces that St. Miguel has arrived. Every-one is welcome to greet the saint (personified in the Obeah-man) in the back room. Immediately, a line forms into the house, and though quite long, moves quickly along. I take a place in line, and soon find myself face-to-face with the Obeah-man, seated at the edge of the official rocking chair from which he greets the guests—some with a single handshake, others with a double. Around his head is wrapped a checkered piece of red and green cloth, knotted in the front. Around his shoulders is draped a larger piece of the same cloth. The checkered clothing, like the cigar, alerts ritual partici-pants that the Obeah-man has formally become St. Miguel.

When it is my turn to greet the Obeah-man I nervously extend my right hand. To my surprise, he takes my hand in his own, yet does not immedi-ately let go. He gazes at me through expressionless eyes, and then takes my left hand as well, creating a crisscross of arms. The Obeah-man pulls me toward him, outlines the symbol of the cross on his chest with our entwined hands, then individually shakes each hand again, first the right, then the left. It is an acknowledgment that St. Miguel has accepted my presence at the Tambú event. As I return to my seat, it becomes apparent that others, in seeing St. Miguel's outward acceptance of me, grow more comfortable with my presence. As I sit down, many offer quiet nods of recognition, smiles, even handshakes.

Following these initial introductions, the second phase of the ritual be-gins, with participants invited to meet individually with the Obeah-man. During this period, devotees consult with St. Miguel in privacy, asking for general or specific questions, guidance, and blessings. While waiting their turn to meet with the saint, some may quietly visit with persons seated next to them; or they may sit in meditative silence, eyes closed, hands lying mo-tionless on their laps. Others, however, congregate in the front room, where they watch or dance to the Tambú music. Although some may enter a trance state during the dance, possession is not vital to attaining spiritual gratifica-tion. As an Obeah-man later explains, "We dance out our problems at Tam-bú." For most, it is the mere physical activity of dance that brings atonement. He later adds, "For those who can't dance, they will live with great difficulty" (Alwin, personal communication, December 29, 2001).

It is interesting to me that many who did enter their own trance during that evening's Tambú did not necessarily adopt the spirit of St. Miguel. De-spite the fact that an event may be organized specifically around a particular saint, possession, when it occurs, may come in the form of any spirit or deity. Many devotees come to develop a personal relationship with a single deity or ancestral spirit during their lifetime. Most come to know their chosen spirit intimately, and come to share their individual likes and dislikes, tem-perament and traits, and so forth. Considered an integral part of a devotee's life, this chosen deity or ancestor may communicate with the individual through dreams or other means. Considered the most revered avenue of contact, though, is the ritual of trance or possession. Tambú events such as this celebration, then, become the most desired forum through which devotees will remember and celebrate their relationships with their chosen deities and spirits.

One woman attending the evening's Tambú confides in me that, through the years, she has developed a spiritual relationship with an Arawak ancestor, born on Curaçao, who had escaped to Venezuela when the Dutch arrived in the early seventeenth century. This Arawak spirit, the woman informs me, continues to reside in Venezuela, like the many other spiritual beings conjured through Tambú, who travel back to Curaçao now and then in order to take part in Tambú gatherings. This woman describes the Arawak ancestor's physical appearance as a beautiful, light-skinned woman with long black hair and a smile that she wears carefully. She also describes her personality to me in great detail: the ancestor's great beauty, it seems, is secondary to her admirable character, replete with a revered determination and sense of leadership. This ancestral spirit, having visited the woman through auspices of trance, causes her to leave this event energized by and thankful for the experience. On her way out, she shares with me that her chosen spirit "is a very strong woman. And I learn a lot about life from her."

When everyone has returned to the garden for the second phase of the Tambú, the adoration table host serves dinner; everyone partakes now of stew meat, rice, potato salad, and greens. Plates are handed to each participant, accompanied by bottles of beer or glasses of whiskey or lemonade. As I join in eating, Rosalia points to the doorway where three people—two men and one woman—stand, smoking cigars. "They are also involved in Tambú," Rosalia explains, indicating that their cigars are clues. Their added attendance at this particular ritual is a tribute to the great popularity of the residing Obeah-man.

As I learn from Rosalia, the most acclaimed Obeah-men and -women enjoy high respect in the Tambú community, which is a compliment not only to their religious authority, but also to their strength in character and intelligence. To be a great Obeah leader, one must exhibit wisdom both in how one directs one's own life as well as how one advises others to live. An Obeah leader may expect questions ranging from money and politics to society and love. It is the Obeah leader's responsibility to know exactly who to summon in the spirit world in order to attain the right answers. Helpful Obeah-men and -women will also be well versed in herbal healing—able to quickly diagnose physical and spiritual ailments; able to prescribe the right

teas to relieve maladies, from indigestion to headache pains; able to construct proper charms that, when worn around the neck, will counteract the
curses imposed by enemies.

Rosalia and I are motioned by the Tambú host to meet personally with
St. Miguel, who greets us in the body of the Obeah-man with handshakes,
saying we are his "special guests" this evening. He also offers us personal
guidance, recalling events from our pasts and listing individual obstacles we
currently face. He ends the conversation by offering a plan through which we
each can attain success in our lives. I self-consciously excuse myself, consent-
ing to give Rosalia privacy as he continues his conversation with St. Miguel.

One by one, all participants are invited to conduct individual meetings
with the saint, but on the stroke of midnight the Tambú abruptly ends. September 29 is set aside to honor St. Miguel, and once that day is finished, so
too is the celebration. Just prior to midnight, another line forms into the
back room. Before the participants leave, each first offers his or her final
regards to St. Miguel, and then asks his permission to exit. When I arrive
at the back room, I see the Obeah-man standing upright, shoulders pulled
back, his arms tightly crossed behind his back. He looks much different from
the man I had met earlier. "He has transformed into another deity," Rosalia
whispers, although which deity's spirit the Obeah-man has now specifically
adopted, Rosalia is not certain. Yet, the difference in the Obeah-man's personality and appearance is quite evident. In discussing his transformation
with Rosalia later that week, I learn that a devotee most likely had requested
guidance demanding the knowledge of more than one deity. Obligingly, the
Obeah-man then summoned further assistance from the larger spirit world.

As Rosalia and I leave the ritual this night and walk slowly back toward
his car, I feel a surprising sense of ease. The participants at the event have
been so open toward me with their feelings regarding Tambú. Suddenly the
warnings and misgivings my Curaçaoan friends had expressed before the
ritual come flooding back over me—admonitions I knew revealed miscon-
ceptions that compelled the Tambú participants themselves to keep their
connections a secret. But by degrees that night, the participants have begun to feel safe enough to reveal them to me. I leave enthusiastic and eager,
having witnessed a firsthand recreation of African history—a clue to the
Curaçaoan past for which I had long searched. Through music and dance I,
too, have been transported to a former time, and while there I manage to jot
down observations and impressions. Later, looking over my notes, I recall

Rosalia's advice: "Write down everything! What you see, the smells—everything has a scent. What do you smell? Write down the colors, how they make you feel. Write down everything!" Thanks to Rosalia's advice, I come away with a personal list of retrieval cues—ones to which I am able to return and activate my own Tambú memories.

Not everything about attending my first Tambú turned out so positively! The very next morning, in fact, I experienced a surprise. Before attending the ritual, my landlady and I had enjoyed a congenial relationship—in fact, I had counted her among my biggest supporters. Even now I remember with gratitude how she helped me hunt down phone numbers of people she believed could assist me. Before the Tambú, our morning encounters were marked with friendliness, with her flinging open her door, ushering me in to enjoy morning tea with her and her husband. However, the morning after the ritual it was obvious how much her attitude toward me had changed. Now the door is cracked ever so slightly, revealing just the shadow of my landlady's face. Her normally jolly voice is quiet but firm as she tells me, "You must move out of the apartment."

I stand there motionless for a time, then knock again, and ask for an explanation. Eventually, her head pokes through cautiously. "You now embrace evil," she states. "You are evil and low class. And you will bring bad luck to me and my family if you remain here." Remorselessly she adds, "You are no longer welcome here." I later learn that my landlady, like so many others, does not profess to believe in Tambú; yet also like many others, my landlady prefers not to test fate. "I know my people," she says, "and I know they will not visit any store that has a reputation for Tambú." She also expresses fear for her son who, she is sure, will face discrimination at school if she allows me to continue to stay after having attended a Tambú ritual. "No parent will want their child to socialize with a low-class family," she explains.

That morning I understand for the first time why the Tambú ritual exists in such guarded secrecy. I have come to experience firsthand the consequences of being too frank about one's Tambú participation, and that has exacted a high cost—in my case, a place of residency. As a practical matter, I resolve thereafter to join the ranks of those who keep their appreciation for Tambú secret.

I return to my research somewhat reticently, wiser yet admittedly frustrated. Trying to make sense of Curaçaoan society's conflicting attitudes toward Tambú has been like assembling a jigsaw puzzle with no clear picture for a guide. Still, after substantial maneuvering, some of these puzzle pieces have begun to fit. The picture of Tambú that eventually begins to emerge depicts the very contradictions that present the best clues to piecing together understanding—not only of Tambú, but of the Afro-Curaçaoan people themselves.

Clap Your Hands!
Bati Bo Mannan!

The past continues to speak to us. But it no longer addresses us as a simple, factual "past." —STUART HALL

Yamada: The Call

A friend recently returned from a visit to Curaçao, eager to share his experiences. He had attended a folkloric show at his hotel, a program advertised as a dedication to the island's representative musical rhythms. Taped music filtered out onto the outdoor pool-turned-stage, with a lone musician, a young boy, playing the *wiri* as accompaniment. A troupe of three couples performed a variety of dances, "including the Tambú!" my friend enthusiastically added. His description, however, recalled a comical drama involving two men vying for the affections of a single woman. At best, it was loosely reminiscent of the *kokomakaku* stick dance. One of the men danced with the woman, while the other paced the sidelines. Following several futile attempts at cutting into the dance, he left the stage, coming back moments later with a small stick, which he flung wildly about. Now armed, he managed to break the dancing couple apart, a victory, however, that was short-lived. His adversary, having briefly left the stage, returned with his own stick. Back and forth, the scene continued, with the men leaving, one by one, and returning each time with larger and larger sticks. Finally, at the song's end, the men both appeared with machetes. The parody brought the audience to laughter, yet the concierge assured my friend that this was "a common practice in Tambú." The evening ended with a fire-eating performance, which, too, was passed off as Curaçao custom. My friend's testimony introduces yet another type of modern Tambú: the folkloric, and brings up interesting complexities regarding the appropriation (and misappropriation) of culture.

The folklorization of Tambú began soon after the 1969 May Movement, when well-intentioned "culturalists" fought to organize formal performances of Tambú as a way to affirm Curaçao's African cultural personality. Its evolution derived from the inalienable need to document, preserve, and celebrate history. Undertaking this responsibility were local anthropologists, archeologists, writers, musicians, and visual artists. They stepped in as interested parties, but quickly became designated caretakers, the "unofficial" spokespeople of Tambú. Local ownership and decision making were pushed to the sidelines, as the collective forces of these culturalists reconfigured Tambú into a fixed form, reshaping it through personal and interpretive efforts. The folkloric version of the ritual emerged as a complex—even contradictory—interplay of cultural projections that, ironically, deepened divisions within Curaçaoan society, ultimately dashing the hopes of culturalists that Tambú would unite the Afro-Curaçaoans.

Folklorization is a process, common to many contested cultural fields, that takes locally held and practiced cultural forms and standardizes, homogenizes, and places them into the public domain beyond the control of the local community. It is a process that, in the Caribbean and on Curaçao in particular, has tended to forge national discourses, focused often on taming or managing "unwieldy" or divisive cultural practices. This attempt at managing and standardizing local practices has led also to a kind of silencing or marginalization of certain elements of indigenous practice so that politically productive elements are played up and other elements are sidelined. Rendering the local "exotic," for example, is one way in which this process of selecting and sifting was achieved. On Curaçao, the folklorization of Tambú was that process by which a quite rigid distinction was drawn between public (officially sanctioned) cultural and the local community-based religious practices of Tambú. Hence, folklorization here represents a process by which certain national-official agendas are worked through, sometimes (and on Curaçao quite often) leading to the marginalization of older and more integrated cultural practices.

In its role as folklore, Tambú became "public memory," pressed into the impossible goal of representing Afro-Curaçaoan culture for an entire community that was itself diverse in terms of class, social status, cultural affiliation, and political interest. The Tambú generated a variety of opinions, and was pulled in different directions, used by some to promote homogeneity, and by others to articulate heterogeneity, to legitimize, and to contest, all in the effort to fill the widening gap between political authority and individual and group interests. Adding to the complexities was Tambú's original role as sacred ritual. When a religious form is turned into folklore, it adapts to mundane contexts and is forced into self-reinvention through the creation of new and unfamiliar secular performance spaces.

In the 1970s, tourism became an increasingly important factor in Curaçao's economy—second only to the oil industry. Cruise ships were making Curaçao a regular port of call, leaving passengers wandering Willemstad streets for a day or an evening; the Dutch-owned KLM Airlines initiated daily non-stop flights to Curaçao from Amsterdam, with many Dutch travelers staying at island resorts or hotels for weeks at a time. Staged reenactments of Tambú were suddenly sought by hotel owners wanting to provide sightseers with opportunities to view the island's culture. Programmed with other Curaçaoan music traditions, including the Antillean waltz and *Seú,* and advertised as part of a "Cultural Show" meant to entertain at area hotels, resorts, and cruise ships, Tambú had found a new market.

As became general practice, dancers in "Cultural Shows" performed to taped accompaniment, and wore costumes meant to evoke the years of slavery: women would be adorned in tightly wrapped cloth, opened scarves tied around their waists; men would wear knee-length white pants with matching jackets, belted with brightly colored cloth. These now commercial dance forms existed to arouse audiences and hold their interest by nostalgically recalling an imaginary time gone by. Generally, the Tambú was danced with overtly sexual movements emphasizing the hips and lower body. Routines typically ended with one woman, hips swinging, rear end extruded upwards, brushing backwards into a male dancer who, in response, exaggerated a fall to the ground. On cue, the tourists would then laugh and applaud at the caricatured movements, seemingly content with this "folkloric" attraction. Tambú in this commercialized form assumed its value precisely because it embodied exactly what many tourists sought when they visited the Caribbean. When re-created in an archetypal repre-

Figure 5.1. Tambú performance for tourists at area hotel. The drummer seated in the background is playing a *Seú* water drum—not a Tambú drum. Photo: Curaçao Historical Archives, 1972.

sentation of the primitive, the erotic, and the exotic, this version of Tambú carried tourists deep into a tropical sensuality, where melody seemed secondary to rhythm and where sexual taboos appeared to be given license.

In being linked to profit making and consumerism, this new Tambú turned history into a saleable commodity. Yet any concern for tradition in the manner in which Tambú would relay this history was considered secondary to the goal of entertainment. The effects these performances had, not only on the people visiting Curacao but also on those living on the island, were far-reaching. Not only did hotel versions of Tambú play a substantial role in shaping the way "Africa" was perceived among the tourists, they also reaffirmed how many Afro-Curaçaoans had already come to imagine "Africa" to be.

Figure 5.1 is a photograph of a Tambú performed at a local hotel during the 1970s. Although this event was presented as a Tambú, the picture of the accompanying instruments, interestingly, shows that no tambú drum was used. Instead, the Seú water drum served as accompaniment, demonstrating just how far removed the tourist versions of the ritual could be from the original.

When my research for this book began some fifteen years ago, Rene Rosalia was a Ph.D. student at the University of Amsterdam. Today, however, he serves as director of the Department of Culture on Curaçao, where he is personally committed to protecting Tambú. Under his guidance, Tambú has been reaching some level of acceptability—when performed as folklore (outside of its ritual context). Tambú folkloric performances have become more frequent, yet carefully packaged in ways that, deemed "more respectable," could better compete commercially with other art forms on the island. By maintaining fixed choreography and Western-devised concepts of musical merit, it was believed Tambú could replace derogatory Curaçaoan attitudes toward African culture with a more positive evaluation. "Tambú is something to be proud of," was Rosalia's response to questions about his approach to bringing the ritual into mainstream consciousness through folkloric events (Rosalia, personal communication, January 5, 2002).

While the motives to make Tambú more compatible with other art forms may have been guided by admirable intentions, the outcome actually has been conflicting definitions of "good" and "bad" art. Compliments of "a good performance" or criticisms of "a bad performance" currently follow folkloric events, with reviews gauged by criteria far removed from those traditional to Tambú. The two folkloric Tambú forms, though very different in content and aim—one organized to preserve history, the other to promote tourism—collapsed into one hybrid construct, as the dances from both types were now expected to meet dramatic choreographic standards, and singing and drumming styles were expected to conform to technical excellence and virtuosic brilliance. Falling short of these expectations immediately consigned the folkloric event—be it at a museum or a hotel—to the category of "bad" art.

The Tambú, no longer structured around local histories and conflicts, is frozen, to be viewed and watched, with little or no opportunity for public participation. Whether seated in a museum or lounging at the Marriott Hotel, audiences are provided the same extraordinary opportunity to revel in an "African" history unfolding from the safety of their seats. The real and the imagined, the familiar and the unfamiliar collide as these audience members must interpret the island's historical narrative through a spectacle of technical virtuosity, ornate costumes, and added folkloric "effects." Difficult questions are raised by this, not least how Afro-Curaçaoans will come to understand their culture through these reimagined performances, and how visitors to the island might assess African-based cultures in general after watching these staged versions.

These re-stagings of folklorized Tambú also tell us something about the hierarchy of values attached to indigenous cultural practices on Curaçao and other colonial spaces. As we have seen, of particular importance in coming to understand the contested field that is Curaçaoan identity are those parts of public discourse that deal with an imaginary Africa or Africanness. In this regard, folklorized Tambú may well be part of a concerted effort to construct a national discourse, but it is also marked deeply by those practices that sought to marginalize, or even force underground, anything connected to Africa. Hence, the national discourse that has grown up around Tambú emerged as an ambivalent and conflicted one.

Afirmashon: The Response

I attend a "Cultural Show" at the *Hotel van der Velk* (located in downtown Willemstad on the Punda side, recently renamed the Plaza Hotel) in 1997. The audience is drawn primarily from the white Dutch staying at the hotel—they conveniently fit the event in between "happy hour" and a midnight scuba-diving tour. A group of young Afro-Curaçaoans serve as the evening's performers, who, billed as "The Van der Velk Dancers," arrive in costume, greeting audience members with nods and smiles. A makeshift stage is quickly created when performers push several tables and chairs to the sidelines. One man, who later introduces himself as the group's sound engineer, is busily setting up a small cassette tape player, pulling the device as far out toward the audience as the extension cord will allow.

Dances are announced in Dutch by the sound engineer prior to each performance. The Antillean waltz, the Curaçaoan *tumba*, local hybrids of the Venezuelan *gaita* and Dominican *merengue*, and the Tambú make up the evening's program. Each dance is carefully choreographed with coordinated spins and leg lifts. Some, including the Tambú, integrate bits of theater into the performance, the Tambú replete with an expected sexual pantomime.

Although individual dancers in this weekly scheduled show may change from performance to performance, the routine and costumes remain consistent. "We practice long hours so that we can learn to dance together . . . to move like one dancer," one of the young female performers explains to

Figure 5.2. Musical transcription of *Yama Áwaseru òf lòs Nubia*. Transcription by the author, taken during a live performance, Lionel, August 19, 1997.

me directly following the show. A man from the troupe quickly adds, "We want to show [the tourists] that we have good dance training on the island." By dancing in precise synchronization, "we make the Tambú dance more respectable."

When questioned further about Tambú, the dancers look at one another in uncomfortable silence. "Why would you want to know about Tambú?" one dancer finally asks. "I don't know anything about it," another states, waving good-bye as she quickly packs up her things. One last performer offers the now common warning, "Tambú is bad. You must be careful. It is best to just stay away." I am not surprised at their reactions, and return to my seat to collect my belongings. However, minutes later, the sound engineer is leaning over me. "I have a friend who plays drum for Tambú," he says softly, adding, "he's playing at the museum at the end of the month." Taking my notebook, he jots down his friend's information—phone number and address—careful to explain that it is the Department of Culture that hires him to perform Tambú at these events. "My friend doesn't believe in Tambú. He's a Christian."

My phone call with the drummer, who goes by the name of Lionel, goes well. The museum event, he explains, is a closed affair. However, I am invited to attend a rehearsal scheduled a few days prior to the event. I eagerly accept. Lionel is performing with several members from the contemporary Afro-Curaçaoan ensemble *Issoco,* which is known throughout the island for its edgy lyrics and strong commitment to African-based music forms. "*Mas Aggressivo!*" is the name of *Issoco*'s most recent hit. "Get aggressive!" the singer shouts at the start of the song. "Let's get very aggressive!" The song was banned from being played on local radio stations soon after its release. However, it continued to garner a large fan base as part of a youth-supported cultural underground, played at music clubs after business hours, when doors were locked and shutters tightly closed.

I walk toward Lionel's home, an impressive white brick building he inherited from his parents. The front door is open, and I walk inside, aware the rehearsal is already in session. Upon seeing me, the musicians stop and disperse to the sidelines, content to take a short break over a glass of whiskey. Only Lionel remains. "I play *Yama Áwaseru òf lòs Nubia* for you," he says, motioning for me to take a seat in the corner. Yama Áwaseru òf lòs Nubia, the music played for the purpose of bringing rain, is part of the program Lionel will play at the museum. His opening solo drum slaps immediately

Figure 5.3. A staged *Paranda di Tambú,* performed in Otrobanda during the 2001 Tambú Season, as part of an afternoon cultural event organized by Rosalia. Photo by author.

draw me in, and I stand transfixed not only by the *tambúrero's* masterful technique, but by the eye contact he maintains with me throughout his solo.

An accomplished musician, Lionel is well versed in the historical and cultural background of his art, which he views from a modern perspective. In an interview, to occur several years later, Lionel explains his involvement in Tambú in this way: "I like to play Curaçao's African music. I may not follow the religion of Tambú, but this does not mean I do not appreciate Tambú music" (Lionel, personal communication, August 17, 2003). Frequently sought out to perform with folkloric groups as well as sacred ritual ensembles, Lionel is a masterful drummer. During our interview, he discloses the interesting fact that while most performances of Yama Áwaseru òf lòs Nubia are commissioned for educational purposes, occasionally he is still hired to perform for the fundamental purpose of producing rain. "Just last week I played a Tambú for rain," he explains. Ironically, the individual who hired Lionel is no farmer, though. It seems a local merchant arranged a serious performance of Yama Áwaseru òf lòs Nubia out of fear that an extended bout of dry weather might hamper his tourist business. Asked to comment

Figure 5.4. Photograph of *Grupo Trinchera* performing at an indoor *Paranda di Tambú*, organized by Rosalia (2001). PHOTO BY AUTHOR.

on ornamentation, Lionel has this to say: "When you play the Tambú to bring rain, you use your drum to speak to the clouds." As he puts it, "You must have the freedom to take the conversation wherever it may go. That is why there is much improvisation in this Tambú" (ibid.).

An example of Yama Áwaseru òf lòs Nubia, played by Lionel (in 1997), is transcribed in figure 5.2. It begins with four elongated rolls representing "sounds of thunder way in the distance" (ibid.). Brief, accelerated phrases lend a rhythmic urgency to the musical line until, in a sudden shift, the elongated rolls return. The following quick triplet figures "represent rainfall. The thunder has come, the lightning has come; now it is time for rain" (ibid.). The Tambú finishes with more elongated rolls leading to a single short accented drum hit to punctuate the end of the piece. As with most Yama Áwaseru òf lòs Nubia, Lionel's version is played with considerable rubato. Can performing a form of Tambú really bring rain? For Curaçaoan musician John James Willekes, the answer is obvious: "Let me just tell you that they don't play this Tambú type any more. And I don't see rain! So what do *you* think?" (personal communication, August 13, 1997).

Rosalia, as director of the Department of Culture, schedules the majority of folkloric Tambú events during the Tambú Season, when legal restrictions against it are relaxed, giving "my office more opportunities to hold Tambú" (Rosalia, personal communication, December 30, 2001). Through

Figure 5.5. Photograph of Tambú drummer and *chapi* musicians, performing at the indoor *Paranda di Tambú*, as part of the event organized by Rosalia (2001). Chapi musicians were invited periodically throughout the event to participate on stage with *Grupo Trinchera*. While the Tambú drummer and a few of the chapi musicians in this photo are regular members of *Grupo Trinchera*, several of the chapi musicians pictured here were invited guests. Off to the sidelines, away from the stage, stood rows of additional chapi musicians who would play along. PHOTO BY AUTHOR.

his efforts, Rosalia has resurrected several traditional Tambú types, which are then performed during the allotted season. *Paranda di Tambú* (translated as "Tambú Parade") is one such example. Distinguished by participants marching between locations to the rhythms of Tambú (see fig. 5.3), the Paranda di Tambú was used by the Africans during slavery as a vehicle for creating a sense of community, a role that Rosalia explains can benefit Afro-Curaçaoans today. "Slavery made the Africans a fragmented people. . . . In the twenty-first century, Afro-Curaçaoans remain a fragmented people. But, just like Tambú united our ancestors during slavery, [Paranda di Tambú] can unite us again" (ibid.).

I attend a Paranda di Tambú organized by the Department of Culture over the Christmas holidays in January 2002. The event does not involve movement from one location to another, nor does it take place outdoors. Although adver-

Figure 5.6. Audience members dancing at the indoor *Paranda di Tambú* event (2001). Photo by Ibrahim Lucas.

tised as a Paranda di Tambú, the event occurs entirely indoors and within one site: a clubhouse made up as a facsimile *hòfi*, its walls painted to represent a tropical outdoor setting. The event is largely organized by Rosalia, and features his ensemble, *Grupo Trinchera* (see figs. 5.4 and 5.5). Several of my Curaçaoan friends refuse to attend this event despite its being advertised as a "cultural affair," and try hard to convince me not to go, with the now familiar warnings: "Tambú is not something to play around with." "Don't go near it!" (Liesje, personal communication, January 3, 2002). One friend repeats the cautionary words her priest shared with the congregation just the week before: "Good women do not go to Tambú," she states flatly, adding, "if you go, just promise me you will not dance" (Layla, personal communication, January 2, 2002).

As the event unfolds, participants gather for the traditional dancing away of the old year's bad luck (see figs. 5.6 and 5.7). Some in attendance are obvious believers in the religious precepts of Tambú, but most appear to be there strictly to connect with historical tradition or, as one participant explained, "to enjoy the company of friends." The manner of dress varies from traditional-looking African print dresses and shirts to jeans and T-shirts. Individual wooden chairs are arranged into rows encircling the large dance area, and a live Tambú band performs on a makeshift stage. A number of singers stand in a single long row at the front, each with an individual microphone. The single drummer sits toward the back of the stage, framed by several musicians playing the traditional iron *herú*. One wall is hung with

Figure 5.7. Audience members dancing at the indoor *Paranda di Tambú* event (2001). Photo by Ibrahim Lucas.

numerous pictures of Curaçao's most famous Tambú singers and with typed pages explaining Tambú history, all carefully framed and neatly arranged. Along another wall several tables are set to serve local snacks; others offer beer and whiskey.

From the start, it is clear that everyone present has come prepared to dance. Adhering to strict Tambú tradition, individuals only dance during the appropriate sections, and move in pairs, arms raised, dancing with one foot grounded, the other stomping in tempo. I ask several in attendance if they believe they are actually dancing away last year's *fuku,* but most respond with laughter. The common reply is, "I don't believe in fuku!" One participant explains, "I dance because it is part of my history." Another adds, "I just like to dance Tambú. It is a fun dance and it is good exercise!" Interspersed among the audience are a few well-respected Obeah-men. One sits in the back, in meditative pose, dutifully shaking hands with admirers. Another, conspicuous in his all-white suit, buoyantly dances the entire event, occasionally going into mild trance states.

For some, the Paranda di Tambú performances are seen merely as a seasonal activity, repeated out of tribute to tradition, just another "way of celebrating a holiday," says one musician. "You know, to be with family. It definitely is not to get rid of fuku!" He adds, "To think that music can get rid of bad luck is nonsense" (Walter, personal communication, August 10, 1997). Fanny Arvelo Salsbach recalls attending a Paranda di Tambú event over fifty years ago—a time when the religious Tambú was not as scrutinized as it is today. "If you knew where to look, it was easy to find Tambú" (personal communication, August 16, 1998). Salsbach recalls that arrangements for Paranda di Tambú were traditionally shared via word of mouth. She describes joining the parading Tambú group as it congregated in downtown Willemstad after work let out one New Year's Eve. "After work I began walking with some friends, and we walked all the way to the opposite end of the island . . . singing, dancing, and celebrating the New Year," she recalls. "We walked all the way to the Bandabou beach. When we got there, we took our shoes off—our feet were tired and sore! And we jumped into the sea. That was a great celebration! . . . Every New Year's, there were several Tambú parades going on [that] I would sometimes attend—I don't believe in Tambú, and never have. But if me going to Tambú brings me good luck, so be it" (ibid.).

Dancing away fuku on New Year's Eve has emerged as another tradition Rosalia has tried to resurrect as director of the Department of Culture. For several years now, he has organized an annual staged Tambú in the central park of the Otrobanda neighborhood of downtown Willemstad on December 31. I attend one such event in 2001. A large stage is erected, and at each corner stand large loudspeakers. To the right of the stage a sagging tent is packed with lines of chairs. At the tent's center, two particularly tall and plush chairs are reserved for the visiting Catholic bishop and Curaçao's governor. The rest of the chairs accommodate the general audience, and are arranged in tight theater-style rows. The chairs are set up very close to the stage, allowing very little room, in order to discourage potential dancing. Individuals who attend the Otrobanda performance do so solely as spectators.

From the start of the program, alternating Tambú groups take to the stage, each congregating around the single drummer, with several percussionists stridently striking iron instruments to provide counterpointed rhythms made ever more piercing by the sound system. Singers equipped with individual microphones provide occasional added hand claps, and at appointed times respond in dance. Although the majority of the Tambú performers wear common street clothes, a few don traditional costumes—flowing skirts for women, knee-length pants for men. Together they move in well-rehearsed linear formations.

Between Tambú performances, older educators (including senior Curaçaoan anthropologists, archeologists, and historians) take the stage to offer lengthy speeches meant to instill pride and knowledge about Curaçao's neglected African past. As the clock nears midnight, attention shifts to the arrival of prominent community members and government officials, who slowly assume their assigned seats. One by one, each walks to the front podium and offers a few short words of acknowledgment. The celebration corresponds little to the traditional *Manda Fuku Bai*. Instead, it is the product of a creative collaboration between politicians, religious leaders, and educators. The audience attending the annual event remains generally small, and visitors clearly outnumber local Curaçaoans. When asked why so few Curaçaoans attend the celebration, one woman responds, "Going to Tambú is a lot like going to a museum. It is good to go and see what is there. You can learn a lot at a museum, but how many people want to go to the same museum, again and again?" (Liesje, personal communication, December 28, 2001).

The speeches continue, and the evening culminates in a prayer offered by an invited bishop (usually from Colombia or Venezuela), who ushers in the New Year with words of prudence and contemplation. Although the word *fuku* is never used, the sentiment remains in the form of the *bendicion* ("blessing") and *felicidad* ("happiness"). The stroke of midnight brings a colorful fireworks display, but as soon as it is over, guests are encouraged to clear the area. "There is no more Tambú until next year," my friend explains, adding, "if we hurry, maybe we can still catch the last part of the salsa show." I leave with my friend that night, to attend the salsa party. As we dance to the Cuban *son* and *guajira* into the early morning hours, Tambú seems but a distant memory.

The status of the folkloric Tambú remains double-edged and is burdened with an essential tension that often comes with ossifying a cultural form. As folklore, Tambú assumes fixity in time, which separates it from the continuity and development of culture. It no longer changes; it no longer adapts to community needs; it no longer speaks to social, political, or religious issues. A nation's need to remember is acknowledged, even as the traditional forms and functions of Tambú are increasingly challenged. Yet in many ways, much of what constitutes a folkloric Tambú performance is so far apart from the ritual's original purposes that the Tambú emerges as more a site of cultural conflict than of collective values and ideals. Tambú audiences increasingly have been replaced by spectators, and performers by entertainers, with Tambú remaining a site of contested and competing meanings.

The spectacularization of Tambú, connected as we have seen to processes of folklorization and attempts to construct a national cultural narrative, works as a means of organizing citizens' relationships with the "island" imaginary. Islands have often generated idealizing political narratives in which hierarchies and class and race contestations are smoothed over or silenced in favor of "official" sanctioned communitarian discourses. The rigid insider/outsider distinctions that continue to operate on the island are rarely acknowledged in these narratives. The shift from religious participation to passive spectator is a shift that is deliberately enacted in this spectacularization. Folklore here stands for administration, and what remains after the enactment of that administration is no less contested: the site of contestation has merely shifted away from conflicts between European and Afro-syncretic cultural practices toward that site at which "official" and "unofficial" Tambú compete for the right to claim Curaçao for themselves.

Come for the Party
Bin na e Fiesta

These tales are all we have of our pasts, and so they are potent determinants of how we view ourselves and what we do.
—DAVID SCHACTER

Yamada: The Call

Each year from November through December official sanctions against the secular Tambú temporarily relax. With radio stations filling air time with Tambú recordings, and parties enjoyed across the island without guest permits, the holidays have become unofficially known as "the Tambú Season." Contemporary Tambú has become a commercial affair: modern Curaçaoan audiences comprise anyone with the money to purchase popular recordings, or those who eagerly await the latest seasonal hits to reach the airwaves. Sharing neither social nor cultural bonds, these listeners often lack understanding of the ritual's traditional purposes. Nor are modern audiences bound to any reciprocal responsibilities: when Tambú Season draws to a close, they are free of further commitment for another year. The season is over and the ties that bind the Afro-Curaçaoan community together loosen, returning them to a globalized space in which their specificity is more distant, their shared memories less easy to recall, their sense of self more diffuse.

Remembering and forgetting, knowing and unknowing: as if mirrored in the annual cycle of on-and-off permission, Curaçao has had to endure the vicissitudes of changing official attitudes to Afro-syncretic cultural practices, with Tambú standing as a model. And this cycle brings a particular quality to the ways in which Curaçaoans access and recall their identities. For some, Tambú represents a seasonal space in which to encounter Curaçaoan pasts; for others, as we shall see, it is merely a seasonal party music with little beyond its pleasure-seeking connotations. Indeed, the commercialization of Tambú plays this out in quite telling ways, emphasizing precisely what is contentious about Tambú: on the one hand, it references a past that, for some members of the authority at least, is better forgotten; on the other, it restages the very danger that commercialization promises (but often fails) to assuage.

Many Tambú musicians have come to measure success in terms of financial profitability. From that perspective, the most successful Tambú band is the one that most wholly caters to mainstream expectations. As George Lipsitz reminds us, "Rarely do we ask about the origins and intentions of the messages we encounter through the mass media. Sometimes we forget that artists have origins or intentions at all" (1990: 5). Critics of Tambú's success within the popular genre decry the playing down of the ritual's historical roots. However, while Tambú composed for popular mass consumption may work to disconnect Afro-Curaçaoans from their traditions, it actually works to unite audiences on another level—namely as consumers. As the Tambú singer Pincho explains, having a designated season "keeps Tambú alive; how can that be bad? Think of the alternative" (personal communication, December 29, 2001).

Relegating Tambú to the holiday months has caused the average Curaçaoan to associate the ritual with Christmas—a misappropriation that further threatens Afro-Curaçaoan tradition. Images of presents under the tree and the arrival of *Sinter Klaus* now tend to overshadow its associations with Africa. As one seven-year-old girl explains, "When I hear Tambú I know that Christmas is coming!" She adds that in her mind, Tambú represents "lots of Christmas lights hanging on the trees" (Yomaida, personal communication, August 16, 2003).

Tambú masquerading in the guise of Christmas music epitomizes Curaçao's larger cultural metamorphosis. Whereas early Afro-Curaçaoan slaves embraced Tambú as a link to a remembered Africa, over a century of social evolution since emancipation has realigned the ritual with a specific Western European holiday occasion. Thus distanced from its African roots, Tambú's past yields to the commercial and popular exigencies of the present.

Relaxation of Tambú restrictions for the holiday season is touted by some as an earnest attempt to rectify problems exposed by the May Movement; yet aligning Tambú with Christmas has proven useful to the island's mainstream conservative agenda. Some upbraid the Dutch authorities for purposefully engineering Tambú Season as a way to "keep the Afro-Curaçaoans in their control," explains a local DJ (Rudy, personal communication, November 4, 1995). Others react more positively: "At least for two months, Tambú is receiving some recognition," says a local jazz musician (Wout, personal communication, August 10, 2003). A handyman by day and Tambú singer and songwriter by night, Pincho appreciates Tambú's seasonal popularity, but fears Afro-Curaçaoans may fail to value or even recognize their own culture. Tambú, Pincho fears, is fast becoming "a lost art." He would prefer to "make sure [Tambú] does not die" by extending its popularity to the other ten months of the year. "Tambú deserves to be heard," explains Pincho, who champions extending Tambú's audience to global proportions. "I would like the world to take note of Tambú," he muses, then more realistically admits he would be content "if only more Curaçaoan people would listen to it" (personal communication, December 29, 2001).

While the requirement for guest list submission is temporarily lifted during Tambú Season, the law still requires permits for dancing at Tambú events. Because these dance permits generally take around two months to secure, all Tambú parties demand considerable pre-organization. "The laws have made it impossible for Afro-Curaçaoan people to just say, 'Hey, let's have a party; let's have a Tambú!'" explains Rosalia. He adds, "This has proven very harmful to our people. The Tambú came out of this spontaneity: whenever there was a need or a sorrow, people would respond quickly with a Tambú. . . . It was our medicine. It was our way of healing. Without the spontaneous Tambú, we lost a major part of who we are as a people" (Rosalia, personal communication, August 13, 2000). Spontaneity has not been totally lost, however. When government permits are denied, the Tambú event may still go forward, though now under carefully guarded secrecy. Regarding possibilities for continuing a sacred Tambú tradition, one man, also from the Department of Culture, offers the following explanation: "Tambú permits are hard enough to get if you want to just have a party. So, you can understand that there is no way the government [would] permit . . . having a Tambú ritual!" (Willekes, personal communication, October 3, 1995).

Even if dancing is not to be included, party hosts must be prepared to allow police officers to station themselves at events to ensure that nothing deemed untoward takes place. Even so, many local bars and restaurants throw Tambú parties for their patrons to enjoy popular Tambú recordings, and sometimes live local Tambú bands. One type of venue is provided by the roadside *truk'i pan*. These vehicles are scattered across the island, parking alongside neighborhood streets to serve sandwiches and drinks to local celebrants. Generally open for business from around 9:00 PM to daybreak, they often provide recorded or live Tambú music to customers during Tambú Season.

Owners of roadside snack trucks are hesitant to speak openly about Tambú dancing, and admit that they sometimes are not granted dance permits. Such denials are usually defended on grounds of public safety. Truk'i pan serving impoverished neighborhoods face special scrutiny, and they are notoriously held accountable for any acts of violence occurring in their vicinity. Even following denial of requests for dance permits, truk'i pan owners occasionally may disregard the law. "People come to dance," one owner admits. "If they cannot dance at my place, they will leave and go somewhere where they can dance. I can't afford to lose customers. So sometimes, shall we say, I look the other way when I see people dancing" (Frederik, personal communication, December 30, 2001). Should the authorities ascertain that dancing has occurred without a proper permit, the truk'i pan may be forced to close, and the snack truck's owner may be heavily fined.

Many neighborhoods eagerly await the return of their favorite truk'i pan businesses each holiday season. The neighborhood of Kwartier, for example, supports the "Yolanda Snek," a truk'i pan with a matchless reputation for lively Tambú performances by *Pincho y su Grupo*. The pride of Kwartier, this unsurpassed Tambú band records top seasonal hits every season, rehearsing weekly during the several months prior to Tambú Season on the outdoor terrace of Pincho's home (located in the Kwartier neighborhood) (fig. 6.1).

Pincho y su Grupo is among today's most sought-after seasonal Tambú bands. Pincho composes most of the song lyrics, consciously integrating the familiar themes into his music, boasting, "The people like my music. I talk about things that are important to the people of today—things that they can relate to." Pincho's band became famous during the 1994 Tambú Season with *Hotel 5 Strea* ("Five-Star Hotel"), which remains a cult classic. The album included songs ranging in subject matter from gossip ("Laga, Mi Ta Laga Bo") to competitive banter ("Ata Payo"). Even the album's cover (see fig. 6.2) illustrates the infiltration of pop culture, with *Pincho y su Grupo* photographed behind jail bars (with the jail ironically portrayed as a "five-

Figure 6.1. Pincho in rehearsal, singing with *Pincho y su Grupo* at his home. His use of a microphone reflects Curaçaoans' growing interest in electronically produced Tambú. Photo by author.

star hotel"), with women dressed to party hovering nearby. "Real life is my inspiration. The topics for my Tambú come to me. I do not find the topics—they find me," Pincho confides. "I can be sitting anywhere, and the entire Tambú [text and melody] will just come to me," adding, "if someone has a problem, he might come to me, too, and ask me to write a Tambú about it—a problem with his girlfriend, a problem with his wife, a problem with his job, any problem! And I will write a Tambú on it" (personal communication, January 2, 2002). Tambú has traditionally reflected life's more mundane pursuits, and Pincho's music is no exception: "Since slavery, Tambú shares the stories of the people. What I do is no different . . . the stories of the people might change, but the storyteller does not change. The Tambú singer is still the storyteller" (personal communication, December 29, 2001).

Pincho sees popular culture as a viable avenue for the reestablishment of Tambú as a traditional art form. He is also aware, though, that there is a good deal of money to be made. While *Pincho y su Grupo* continues to "play Tambú because we want to keep our tradition going," he readily admits they do so "because there is a market for it." Pincho's philosophy is that everyone should profit from developing his/her individual talents. "From the doctor to the postman—why not the Tambú musician?" he asks. Pincho sees no conflict between financial success and artistic integrity: "Tambú needs to have an audience," he says, adding that if this means writing for a popular audience, "so be it." Yet Pincho continues to stress that his overriding goal remains "mak[ing] sure Tambú does not die" (personal communication, December 29, 2001).

In testament to Pincho's dedication to the contemporary preservation of Curaçaoan culture, he welcomes adolescents to attend the rehearsals and to discover the established Tambú traditions. Pincho's young niece, who attends many such rehearsals, is already becoming proficient in the basics of traditional Tambú singing. Since women dominated Tambú nearly a century ago, and today just a few women perform as chorus singers (and still fewer as lead singers), Pincho is particularly encouraging of his niece. "She even writes her own songs," he declares proudly.

Beginning drummers and *chapi* players also attend rehearsals, spending the majority of their time sitting on the sidelines, carefully watching and studying. After formal rehearsals, or occasionally during breaks, it is their turn to take the stage. Welcoming the encouragement of the more experienced players, neophytes learn the proper technique for slapping a drum or holding the chapi, and the basics of ornamentation and improvisation. Rene Rosalia's Tambú ensemble, *Grupo Trinchera,* also functions as an appropriate training ground for promising young musicians. Although the group relies heavily on its core of veteran performers, the younger and less experienced are also encouraged to attend rehearsals, where they learn musical and dance traditions from respected elders. Following the time-honored tradition of apprenticeship, these young musicians, when deemed ready, are encouraged to replace more seasoned players during the final few dances of important cultural events, where they get the chance to display their newly acquired skills.

As popular culture, Tambú has become implicated in its own commodification, its audience assembled commercially, its membership bestowed upon all who purchase recordings. Audiences for today's popularized Tambú need neither share a common history nor even necessarily know one another. As a result, they are free from all reciprocal responsibilities as well as any obligations demanded by the traditional ritual. Pop-Tambú audiences unite principally through consumer desire, and with cultural identity and bloodline no longer factors, challenge the very legitimacy of perceived memory and identities inherited from the past.

Although Tambú makes prime radio during the allotted November and December months, only apolitical or non-social compositions will enjoy the privilege of airtime. Such censorship further distances Tambú from its traditional form and purpose. Musicians like Pincho, in order to realize financial success through Tambú performance, end up forming bands that cater to mainstream expectations. Yet Tambú composition and performance

Figure 6.2. The cassette cover to a recent Tambú recording by *Pincho y su Grupo*.

relegated to the level of commercialism do little to further the preservation of cultural memory.

Some Tambú purists remain critical of musicians who, like the members of *Pincho y su Grupo* and *Grupo Trinchera*, teach Tambú technique to young players without instructing them in basic cultural history. As one such chapi musician complained, "These kids who come to rehearsals now and then maybe learn one or two Tambú. And they think they are experts on Tambú?" (Rudsel, personal communication, January 3, 2002). Another chapi player expresses similar concerns: "There is more to Tambú than playing a drum just so, or being able to memorize the words to a Tambú song." He adds, "Tambú is about history, our history, our African history. And that is not being taught to these kids" (Franklyn, personal communication, August 10, 1997). Pincho and Rosalia remain committed despite criticism, quickly pointing out that information on Tambú technique transmitted to young people from committed band leaders, despite obvious shortcomings, is likely to remain the only information they will obtain on their heritage. "School children won't hear about Tambú from their school teachers," Rosalia points out. "There are no classes on Tambú in their schools! In fact, there are no classes in Caribbean history! Or African history!" (personal communication, December 30, 2001). Of course a total understanding of Tambú must certainly involve more than the techniques of singing, drumming, and dancing; yet these basic rudiments, taught by members of bands like *Pincho y su Grupo* and *Grupo Trinchera*, provide students with an educational setting replete with teachers recognized and respected in their field. Criticism notwithstanding, Rosalia, Pincho, and others impart the legacy of Tambú performance to future generations.

Afirmashon: The Response

In 2003, I attend a boisterous Tambú party at a snack truck located near the neighborhood of Santa Maria. The owner, who has secured a dance permit with hopes of providing a live band, instead accommodates the crowd with recorded Tambú music emanating loudly from a large sound system set up on the flatbed of a second truck. A man standing nearby serves as disc jockey, selecting Tambú recordings from a table stacked with small piles of compact discs and cassette tapes. The large, mostly male audience comprises mainly young people in their late teens, and the area is quite dark, with limited lighting from the snack truck and a nearby street lamp casting shadows in haphazard fashion. Having secured the proper permits, the truk'i pan owner provides the audience with a large dance floor. However, a surprising few actually choose to dance. Most stand at the sidelines, eating and drinking, talking and laughing with their friends. The few couples who do dance carefully follow Tambú protocol, swaying in place during the *habrí* section, hips swinging rhythmically to the recorded chapi beat, and immediately switching to the traditional Tambú dance at the start of the *será*. Obviously these young dancers are versed in the aesthetic conventions of Tambú. As the evening progresses, more teenagers arrive, but still only a few dance. Most continue to congregate in groups along the sidelines, the crescendo of their talking and laughing now competing with the loud Tambú music.

Around 1:00 AM, a small group of young musicians arrive, one carrying a *barí*, two others with chapi tucked carefully under their arms. Two more cart in a portable sound system with detachable microphones. I note that one of the musicians looks familiar—a chapi player I had met during a rehearsal at Pincho's home. Their arrival, suggesting the prospect of live Tambú music, brings cheers from the sidelines. The young musicians begin setting up in a corner near the disc jockey, and nearly an hour later commence their first set. Most of the preparation time is spent adjusting the sound system, with the lead singer making several gallant, though unsuccessful, attempts to keep the large crowd quiet long enough for a proper sound check. Hands outstretched, pantomiming surrender in battle, he presently returns to the stage and orders the band to begin. At the first slap of the drum, the audience crowds the dance space.

In addition to couples, numerous single dancers also take to the floor, all eager to participate. Following the rules of proper Tambú dance etiquette, they remain quiet during the habrí section, listening intently to the lead singer. Then, at the start of the será, everyone joins excitedly in dance, immediately energetic, eagerly dancing while keeping time with hand claps. Most of the Tambú songs that evening stick to standard popular themes, like love and betrayal. One popular number is about a man who loves two women—one petite, the other very large. As if on cue, the audience uniformly laughs at the plight of the song's protagonist, who in the end, decides to remain with the larger-built girlfriend because, "If she would decide to sit on me, I would surely die!"

Dancers remain on the floor throughout the set, clapping when songs convey the irony in love, chuckling when details of love turn more sexual in nature, shouting at the start of each será. The audience seems unaware of the band's constant struggle with their sound system. During nearly every song, one musician stands at the back, huddled over the sound board, obsessively twisting knobs and buttons to find what he perceives as a clearer, more balanced sound. Instrumentalists and singers share this pursuit of perfection. If one misses a cue or harmonic change, other band members will shoot them collective glares of disapproval. Short interludes between songs become opportunities for quick reassessment.

The live Tambú performance is in two sets. When the musicians take their break between sets, the disc jockey returns with more recorded Tambú—to which the audience reacts with immediate disinterest, retreating once again to the sidelines to resume their loud talking and laughing. Not until the musicians return for their final set does the audience reclaim the dance floor. "Music can be a verb or noun, depending on its context of performance," Christopher Small explains in *Musicking: The Meanings of Performing and Listening* (1998: 4). The audience's reaction to live versus recorded Tambú presents an effective illustration of *musicking* in action.

The audience has regarded recorded Tambú as tantamount to background music, while live performance immediately ignites animated participation, with rhythm, movement, and text uniting a social community. While the audience may seem pleased with the live band that night, the Tambú musicians themselves appear rather disappointed in their performance. It seems modern Tambú musicians have come to emulate some of the appraisal markers known to performers of Western European music. Many Tambú musicians now aspire toward technical precision and accuracy in their music, and hold precious little patience for any presentation perceived to fall short. Modern Tambú bands have come to place a higher value on refined performance than on the success of the social activity Tambú encompasses.

The apparent antithesis of *musicking*, seasonal Tambú parties, though primarily social events, have profit making at their center. Tradition and culture seem to have capitulated to consumerism and marketing as reasons to celebrate the ritual in the twenty-first century. With radio relentlessly doling out commercialized Tambú music during the allocated season, parties amass large followings among the island's youth. Older Curaçaoans sometimes view these parties as promoting unhealthy activities such as drinking and gambling, or worse still, carousing and fighting. When occasional acts of violence do mar the spirit of Tambú Season, the authorities seem quick to link them to Tambú. As a result, youth participation in the ritual has become linked with connotations of juvenile delinquency. In fact, Curaçaoan youth (as with young people everywhere) often rebel against what they see as the Establishment, eschewing authoritarian rule in favor of discovering their own individuality, or at least a sense of personal identity distinct from that of the older generation. What better arena to display the rebellion of youth than against the backdrop of Tambú—a music held in gravest disdain by their parents? Small wonder Curaçaoan teenagers' testing of the waters often takes the form of attending Tambú parties. Yet as the members of the island's youth grow to adulthood, most come to embrace the standard prescribed philosophy of the island's dominant culture, inevitably assuming the very disdain for Tambú their own elders had displayed in the past.

Because dance permits remain compulsory even during Tambú Season, some Tambú parties are denied permission to include dance. I attend one such private party at which no dancing is permitted. This party is held in the large side yard outside a private home. A number of tables line the sides of the yard, with wooden chairs scattered about. Cords of red and green lights strung from four large trees framing the yard provide a festive atmosphere. Uncertain exactly why a dance permit was denied them, the hosts indicate they suspect inadequate parking facilities. "It is very hard for people to have a party in a residential area," the one host explains. "People can park real crazy, you know? Up on everybody's yard, double-parked on one side of the road. It can be crazy" (Martin, personal communication, January 2, 2002). The female host, along with several of her friends, run to and from the house with plates of food to serve guests. At the back of the yard one long table stands loaded with rum, whiskey, gin, and vodka, along with soft drinks and an assortment of juices. Toward the front, a Tambú band (dominated by young players) performs under a cloth tent.

Since no dancing is allowed, the audience is cast in the role of observers rather than as participants. Most stand watching at the sidelines, quietly listening to the music. I note that some occasional dancing does occur; however, the manner in which the couples dance is no longer recognizable as Tambú. There is no foot stomping, no swinging of the hips. Instead couples hold one another close, slowly swaying back and forth in a manner reminiscent of popular American slow dance. Their minimal movement and slow shuffling feet seem absurdly incongruous against the fast rhythms and energized singing of the band.

As the night progresses, most of the older guests leave and are replaced by a younger crowd. Many are teenagers, seemingly eager to be part of an adult function. The girls wear provocative clothing and makeup associated more often with adult fashion; the boys wear the low-riding jeans, massive gold chains, and colorful baseball caps often associated with the hip-hop styles of the United States. Judging by their dress, these young people seem to be testing out identities of adulthood and independence. To push the envelope further, drinking quickly becomes the focus of the young people's socializing, with many unable or unwilling to indulge in moderation.

Many of my Curaçaoan friends express concern over this party, and attempt to persuade me to stay home. Only after several discussions does my closest friend agree to take me to the party, but makes it clear we cannot be staying long. When the teenagers arrive and make quick lines to the alcohol table, my friend demands we both leave. Although disappointed, I give in to her demand. From there we head over to a jazz club where a mutual friend is performing. But on our way home afterwards, I convince my friend to drive a route that will just take us past the party—I am interested in seeing if the crowd has increased. As we draw nearer, the traffic grows heavier until we can only inch our way along. As we draw near the party location we see flashing red lights, then a number of police officers pulling handcuffed youths into the back of their cruisers. "What's going on?" my friend yells to a passerby. "There's been a shooting!" is the response. My friend now turns toward me, and acerbically reiterates all of her warnings against Tambú and Tambú parties.

Audience members who agree with the perspectives rendered in Tambú song texts can re-create, through dance, the world projected in song; those who disagree, however, are still invited to at least consider the alternative through similar interactive involvement with the singer and the attending musicians. In this way, Tambú's edifying strength lies beyond the textual words, and more in its ability to stimulate empathy and order through the active communication of dance, uniting Tambú singers, musicians, and audience members into an interactive "we." When dance is removed from a Tambú event, another vehicle for creating community is sought.

In retrospect, I continue to compare the two Tambú parties I attended—the one where dance was *not* allowed, and the large gathering at the snack truck, where it *was*. I continue to be struck by the differences, which revolved mainly around the use and misuse of alcohol. Drinking occurred at both parties, and both drew crowds of younger Curaçaoans. Yet it seems to me the audience around the truk'i pan were given the opportunity to participate in a community through Tambú dance, where all seemed to partake eagerly and enjoy the experience. At the second party, where dance was not permitted, however, drinking became the primary communal activity and the primary focus of their interaction as a community.

By mid-January, as staunch legal restrictions against Tambú again fall back in place, the parties featuring Tambú disappear. For the remainder of the year—outside of November and December—Tambú parties remain difficult if not impossible to find on Curaçao. People once again go about their day-to-day lives, most ending their involvement with Tambú until the season rolls around again the following November.

Conclusion: Are You Ready?
Are You Ready to Hear the History
of Tambú?
Conclui: Bo Ta Kla? Bo Ta Kla pa Tende
e Historia di Tambú?

No one can become what he cannot find in his memories.
—JEAN AMÉRY

Yamada Final: The Final Call

Our discussion of the phenomenon known as Tambú, so immediately re-
sistant to disclosure, has been developed in this book to reveal its manifold
transformative abilities. Frequent changes in Curaçao's economic environment, coupled with similar changes in the island's philosophical and political climates, have shaped and informed Afro-cultural adjustments to the
changing esteem in which the dominant society held the black community
and worked to construe Tambú into a multiplicity of types: some with sacred overtones, others more secular in nature. While individually unique,
each maintains a hold on tradition by incorporating similar conventional
elements of musical rhythm, structure, instrumentation, and style.

Tambú constitutes part of a legacy in which Africans throughout the
New World have engaged as a means of cultural survival appropriate to their
environments. Rituals of great variety were created "that were at once new
and immensely dynamic. African in overall tone and feeling, [yet] nonethe-
less wholly unlike any particular African society" (Price and Price 1999: 28).

Donald Hill divides New World rituals into two general types. The first includes those rituals that draw upon the traditions of one particular ethnic group, like "the *Orisha* of Trinidad and the *Lucumi* of Cuba [which] are largely Yoruban," and the seventeen *Nanchons* ("Nations") in Vodou, each "thought to be derived from a separate ethnic group in Africa—Rada, Kongo, Ngo, Ibo, and so on" (Hill 1998: 183). Orisha, Lucumi, and Vodou shared other specific similarities as well: each was restricted to the African gods, who would arrive at the ritual one at a time, each ascribed a distinct musical rhythm, played by an ensemble of three drums.

Hill's second ritual type includes those that reflect the union of many nation groups, like the *Big Drum* of Carriacou, Grenada, "where special rhythms were associated with specific nations" (ibid.: 188); and the carnival of Trinidad, "a symbolic way in which the complex Creole identity is worked out, developed, and refined" (ibid.: 191–192). This second category implies a later development than the first: Orisha, Lucumi, and Vodou are rooted in the early years of slavery, whereas the *Big Drum* evolved in the mid-eighteenth century and the Trinidad carnival in the nineteenth century. Rituals from this second list also follow more secular lines and exclude acts of possession—as Hill points out, the Carriacou people do not consider *Big Drum* a religion, and carnival is uniformly considered "secular popular entertainment" (ibid.: 191).

Placing Tambú within this dual paradigm is problematic. In its unique adoption of the ancestors, the African gods, *and* the creole deities, Tambú unites Curaçao's divergent African presences. Representing, in the words of Hill, a "'hub' of Creoleness," Tambú can be placed as part of the second-mentioned ritual group. At the same time, its religious intent and adoption of possession firmly situates it within Hill's first designated category. Yet, again here, Tambú manages to stand apart. In contrast to Orisha, Lucumi, and Vodou, Tambú utilizes only one ritual drum and welcomes the gods *and* the spirits; deities do not arrive one at a time, but in crowds of eight, nine, ten, or more; and musical rhythm does not dictate deities' arrival, but instead it is Tambú's binary structure that commands their appearance. Why Tambú has emerged and developed so differently advances discussions on history and its impact on ritual development, furthering the premise that New World rituals are powerful models for uncovering the cultural intricacies of African–New World history. As a historically linked ritual in motion, Tambú has acquired multiple attachments: Tambú symbolizes both an African past and a New World reality; it is a religion yet also a party; it provides a sense of community to some, while it remains an object of fear and frustration to others. In its varied manifestations, Tambú represents more a process than a product. It emerges as a system of representations, connected to history through a constellation of factors and forces—not simply a consequence of it.

Within social contexts where displacement created crises of continuity, tradition emanates with a certain urgency, although the exactitude of the referenced past assumes a secondary importance to whatever unification and self-expression past "truths" can provide. In his monumental seven-volume work *Les Lieux de Mémoire* ("The Places of Memory"), Pierre Nora argues that when circumstances force a collapse in tradition, communities necessarily devise new ways of remembering to maintain unity among their members (1984–1992, 1996–1998). In place of actual memories, various cultural expressions or symbolic "places" of collective memory (such as monuments, commemorative ceremonies, or political movements) emerge as the "focal points of . . . national heritage" (Nora 1996: 83). Although *lieux de mémoire* serve as instrumental vehicles for collective memories underpinning social cohesion, Nora stresses that historical continuity is imagined. Ironically, *lieux* become representations of the past, adopting from and adapting to the dominating moral and political values selectively.

A striking example of *lieu de mémoire* is the Tambú, marking the beginning and end of slavery; demonstrating the motivation of an enslaved African people determined to remember; and in some of its modern forms, portraying a commitment by those with no personal memory of Africa to reconstruct perceived ancestral memories. "There are *lieux de mémoire*, sites of memory, because there are no longer *milieux de mémoire*, environments of memory," Nora writes (1989: 7). The diverse groups of Africans on Curaçao were wrenched from individual pasts. Miraculously, Tambú evolved to unite the *milieux* of variegated histories into a private *lieu*, preserving perceived traditions while maintaining collectivity.

Since, according to Nora, the past undergoes a social transformation when it becomes a *lieu de mémoire*, Tambú also provides a compelling lens through which to examine the complex interaction of politics and public opinion in the construction of social memories. Tambú's move from *milieux* to *lieu de mémoire* has been complex, largely because Curaçao has yet to attain economic and political independence from the Netherlands. In efforts to maintain social control, particularly after emancipation, the Curaçaoan government has remained relentless in pursuing the limitation of

Tambú, constant in attempting to eradicate participation through the power of weapons and the threats of imprisonment. The church joined the government's efforts, fighting the ritual with the prospect of improper burial and banishment to Hell. While such sanctions initially did little but push Tambú underground, the continued onslaught understandably has taken its toll—legal persecution against Tambú participants still exists. While Tambú, as *lieu de mémoire*, may have evolved out of a New World quest for history, an attempt by Curaçao's earliest African peoples to transcend the loss of individual memory, its limited usage today means that the memory of Africa faces possible extinction on Curaçao. The implications of this have been far-reaching, digging into the very heart of Afro-Curaçaoan identity.

Indeed, identity emerges as a complex paradigm on the island, representing all the contradictions and complications of the African Diaspora. *"Joe'i Kórsou?"* ("Who is the true Curaçaoan?") is a question that has come under heated debate today, with a wide range of cultural identities currently circulating across the island. "I am Cuban." "I am Brazilian." "I am African, Dutch, Sephardic Jew, Native American!" (De Jong 2006: 24). Admittedly, these diverse concepts of self seem oddly misplaced. Most Curaçaoans I have spoken with have never traveled to the region designated by their assumed identity (nor has anyone in their immediate family). What emerged during the course of our conversations was that Curaçaoan identity is in flux, adjusting to and reconciling a changing Caribbean society, in the end, emphasizing the island's growing cultural heterogeneity. It is an approach to identity that developed so gradually that it became conceived as a natural condition of an accepted part of Curaçaoan life.

As testament to how detachment toward Tambú encouraged a disconnect with Africa, Afro-Curaçaoans prior to the twentieth century closely aligned themselves culturally with the Netherlands. Like other New World colonies, Curaçao adopted polemically based identities during slavery, where "Being Dutch" or "Being African" was the choice. Attitudes changed during the twentieth century, when globalization, experienced through migration, television, and the internet, introduced new representations of identity, presenting Afro-Curaçaoans with new and different ways of life. Issues of personal identity became ripe for challenge and contest as Afro-Curaçaoans exercised the freedom to explore cultures other than Dutch. China, Cuba, India, and Brazil offered a "third option" to the duality of Africa and the Netherlands. Thus were new spaces of belonging pioneered, and alternatives to Dutch colonial expectations acquired. For Afro-Curaçaoans not yet ready to announce to the world: "I'm African!" the new cultural affiliations provided alternative models through which one might proclaim, at the very least, "I'm not Dutch!"

These external geographic locations caught the imagination of Curaçaoans through ritual practice. Specifically, when Tambú's popularity decreased, new identification rituals emerged, commemorating revised "mythic explanations" of a Curaçaoan existence (Kammen 1991: 27). Indeed, rituals may change in terms of form, symbolic meaning, or social effects, with new rituals arising as old ones fade away. Yet, rituals do not simply arise or decline spontaneously. Their evolution or demise is influenced by the society from which they emerge, with the strength of ritual activity lying in the ability to invoke people's beliefs regarding their place in a larger order of things (Bell 1997: xi). Because people are not just slaves of ritual—they are also molders of ritual—the ritual construct represents an ongoing process of social drama, carefully wrapped in webs of symbolism that can be created and altered.

An interesting counterstory can be found in the Afro-Curaçaoan migration to Cuba during the early 1900s, which resulted in the emergence of a ritual disguised as a party. Called *Comback*, it features Cuban music styles popular among Afro-Cuban nationalists during the Afro-Curaçaoan migration, including the *son, guaracha, guajira,* and *danzón*, which had been adopted as markers of personal identity by the Afro-Curaçaoan migrant workers. Played on original 78s (brought into Curaçao by the migrant workers) or performed live by Curaçaoan bands consciously imitating the styles of 1920s Cuba, the *son, guaracha, guajira,* and *danzón* have enabled a Cuban memory to be passed down to younger Curaçaoan generations at *Comback* parties. Participants step to the Cuban rhythms, dancing out connections to a perceived history, using the *Comback* ritual not so much to enact specific origins or to allege authentic folk forms, but to unite the present with the past in a dynamic yet continuous process of collective reinterpretation and reenactment. Through the continued popularity of the *Comback* party, Cuba has flourished as an identity choice, embraced by the young and old alike, by whites and blacks (De Jong 2003b).

While the *Comback* party and accompanying Cuban identity remains popular, of late, a growing number of Curaçaoans have combined ethnicities out of their nation's distinct pluralism to create individualized "hybrid" concepts of self. Among examples I have encountered are "half white Curaçaoan, half Portuguese"; "Curaçaoan-born authentic pure-blood Venezuelan"; and a plethora of other combinations of African, Dutch, Sephardic Jewish, and Native American backgrounds.[1] While historians often see pluralism as a dividing force, splitting populations into separate social enclaves (Hoetink 1958), on Curaçao, blended notions of identity actually promoted social unity, "creat[ing] cultural coalitions that transcend ethnic and political differences" (Lipsitz 1997: 130). This diversity in identity has found common ground in Curaçaoan jazz, a highly stylized and complex form that blends different musical styles—Brazilian, Cuban, Native Amerindian—into a single eclectic style. Put simply, musicians borrow musical elements they believe reflect their chosen geographical regions of origin, and use the jazz concert to "perform" these individualized senses of self.

As example, I share one of the first jazz performances I attended on the island (in 1995). Held on a hot Monday evening in an outdoor café, the event showcased a well-rehearsed ensemble that included bass, saxophone, and piano. "A Night in Tunisia" was playing as I made my way into the audience. The bass player's melodic lines were simple, his motives quite minimalist in character; as he later explained, this musical approach represented his "100 percent Arawak" identity. The pianist's improvisational accompaniment, in contrast, was stylistically reminiscent of Thelonious Monk in its percussive accents and angular phrasing, yet it comprised unusual salsa *montuno* lines; he later confessed that this approach represented a cultural alignment with Cuba. The saxophonist's rhythmic style, with unexpected high-register squeals, suggested avant-gardist Albert Ayler—this musician had developed an African-centered sense of self while living in the United States during the 1960s, and was one of the few on the island to openly embrace an African identity, using jazz to "celebrate my African soul." Over the years, I made numerous such visits to Curaçao's various jazz clubs. By degrees I have begun to perceive that such stylistic elements both defined Curaçaoan jazz, and were a reflection of revised constructions of cultural

1. These ethnic classifications come from an advertisement for Rudy's Grocery Store, taken from the local newspaper *Bala* (October 23, 1992), as cited by Alan Benjamin (2002, 52). "Suriname Chinese-African" was the identity claimed by Curaçaoan Ewald Onga Kwie; "Curaçaoan-born authentic pure-blood Venezuelan" was the identity claimed by Curaçaoan Errol Cova; and "African, Dutch, Sephardic Jew, Native American" was the identity claimed by Rudy Plaate, the owner of the store. The stated intent of the advertisement was Plaate's desire that "all ethnic identities . . . feel welcome at his store" (52). The advertisement serves as written testimony to the wide range of identities existing on Curaçao, as well as the people's own acceptance of their individual differences.

identity. "I know I must have been Brazilian in a past life," one saxophonist conveyed after performing a bossa nova–like improvisation to the Miles
Davis tune "All Blues" (see De Jong 2006: 33). "Venezuela has captured my
soul," said an elderly bandleader, proudly sharing his musical arrangements
of jazz standards, each integrating a different Venezuelan rhythm, like *gaita*,
joropo, and *bambuco* (ibid.).

Exercising identity choices through jazz performance is not limited to
the performing musicians. Audience members, too, are quick to participate.
When they hear a musician playing in a style emulating their own choice
in identity, they stand and cheer. Onlookers who do not hear their choice
in identity may contribute through their own rhythmic responses, tapping
out a Colombian *cumbia* rhythm across the table (if their cultural identity
is Colombian) or hitting a Cuban *son clave* against the side of an available
beer bottle (if their cultural identity is Cuban). In this way, the jazz concert
has emerged as a contemporary ritual of identification. In contrast to the
Comback party, where a single Cuban identity is sought, Curaçaoan jazz cel-
ebrates a variety of identity choices, uniting people who have adopted separate and individual senses of self. Yet, no matter how differently members
of Curaçaoan jazz ensembles (and accompanying audiences) approached
identity, the jazz performances sounded polished and indeed well connected. The ritualistic nature of the Curaçaoan jazz concert shatters the illusion
of separateness on Curaçao, and actually fuses participants into a shared
state of being by affirming a sense of unity among them.

Examining Tambú against the *Comback* party and Curaçaoan jazz
brings the topic of memory and politics to the forefront. The *Comback* party
and the Curaçaoan jazz concert are legal activities. They are allowed to exist
without interference by the church and state; they occur frequently and are
popularly attended. Regular participation means that communal effects can
be met, that the celebrated traditions and perceived memories in both the
Comback and Curaçaoan jazz can be passed successfully from generation
to generation. Tambú, in contrast, lacks social acceptability. As a result, it is
not ongoing; the African pasts celebrated in Tambú are not retold with any
regularity, and its traditions are not readily passed between and among generations. Precisely because of the politics of memory, Cuban culture, as celebrated in the *Comback* party, and the inventive hybrid cultures, recognized
in Curaçaoan jazz, have taken root on Curaçao, whereas African culture has
not. In fact, the further Curaçaoans have distanced themselves from Tambú,
the more out of favor Africa has become.

Afirmashon Final: The Final Response

Selective memory is not always easy to acknowledge or understand, precisely because the selectivity serves a political purpose: usually, to justify the claims of one group over a competing group. Since memory represents a field of contestable meanings, we must consider what may have already been forgotten and why. When commemorative rituals are not firmly embraced, time becomes the enemy of cultural memory: without the opportunity to remember, experiences are inevitably forgotten. Personal recollection reinterprets the past, weaves new life-stories and myths together into new creations. Dan McAdams writes that "The unfolding drama of life is revealed more by the telling than by the actual events told. Stories are not merely 'chronicles,' like a secretary's minutes of a meeting, written to report exactly what transpired and at what time. Stories are less about facts and more about meanings. In the subjective and embellished telling of the past, the past is constructed—history is made" (1993: 28). As a field of contested meanings, memory indicates a cultural community's collective desires, needs, and self-definitions. Memory's fluidity and great importance to a community's existence make it appear fragile, fluid, and changing. This instability raises important concerns about how the past can be verified, understood, and given meaning. We need to ask not whether a memory is true but rather what its telling reveals about how the past affects the present. Answers to these concerns provide insights into how culture functions and how appositional politics engage remembrance.

According to Daniel Schacter, when individual and community needs shift, memory and forgetting respond with predisposed selectivity (1986). Memory, regardless of what is being remembered or by whom, is ultimately retained in bits and fragments of the total actual experience. Furthermore, the act of remembering selectively recalls from among these stored pieces only those actually evoked through the specific stimuli, which Schacter calls "retrieval cues." Afro-Curaçaoan memory has been figured in this book as one of amnesia, emphasizing the apparent ease with which Afro-Curaçaoans forget and rewrite the past. Interestingly, all the Tambú types maintain the same "retrieval cues," which enable each Tambú to connect to ancient antecedents (traditional rhythms, instrumentation, structure, and stylistic features). Yet, while these cues are meant to trigger recollection of memory, the many laws and sanctions against Tambú have actually weakened people's understanding of those cues.

As a result, the "retrieval cues" have adopted new associations or have been reduced to simple cultural motifs, leaving Tambú stagnant, and placing history and memory at odds. Audiences no longer are free to respond to Tambú in their own way. Rather, Tambú responses have been codified and prescribed, dictated specifically by the particular Tambú. Folkloric Tambú demands Afro-Curaçaoans be spectators, watching from the sidelines, appreciating the performance for its cultural or historical significance. The response by party Tambú–goers fluctuates, according to whether or not the party host has secured a dance permit. When the host secures a permit, Afro-Curaçaoans arrive expecting to dance and socialize; yet, when the permit is denied, they arrive equally content to enjoy Tambú as background music, tapping their feet to the ritual beats while sharing drinks with friends. Modern Tambú has assumed a plethora of new meanings, yet it involves a process that appears neither innocent nor objective.

"Tambú is Africa," saxophonist John James Willekes says. It is "our only link to Africa, our link to our history. When we turn our backs on Tambú, we are turning our backs on our history" (personal communication, October 3, 1995). Willekes is concerned that "not enough Curaçaoans really understand that they are an offspring of Africa." Many complain "we have no history here on this island." Agreeing that ongoing colonial policies have made it difficult for a positive African identity to exist, he nods, quickly adding, "Our history is inside Tambú—inside its rhythms, inside its songs, inside its dances." Because of his choice in identity, Willekes says he has faced much opposition, the community reluctant to accept him or his philosophies. "If you say you are African, the people will be hostile to you. That is the way it is on Curaçao. It is crazy, because the people who are the most hostile are the African people on the island. Isn't that some crazy shit?" The Dutch, he explains, "have done a good job at colonizing Curaçao. They didn't stop [with] the land. They went on and colonized our thoughts, our minds. The Dutch convinced us that Africa is bad. And now we are busy trying to convince each other." It is important to note that, by 1999, Willekes had moved to the United States, where he now resides. "Should I ever leave," he prophesied in 1995, "it will be because I am just too tired to keep fighting with people who do not want to hear the truth. I will return someday, when they are ready to listen."

"Tambú is the music of demons," warns an elderly Afro-Curaçaoan woman (Helena, personal communication, August 6, 1998). Opposed to the ritual even during the allotted months of November and December, she explains: "I am a Christian woman. Anyone who even steps foot into Tambú has betrayed God." Her church, like many on the island, imparts a message of concern and alarm, and threatens expulsion to anyone suspected of attending Tambú rituals. Her words seem mirror images of warnings regularly spoken by her priest: "What kind of example do mothers show their children when they dance or sing Tambú?" "Women who attend Tambú are bad women." "What man wants to marry such a woman? I'll tell you! No man—no decent man—will marry such a woman!" As may be expected from these critical warnings, few women currently involve themselves in Tambú. Interestingly, the pregon role was dominated by women during slavery and the years immediately following emancipation. Today, however, the majority of singers are men. In fact, from ritual to folklore and from party to hotel entertainment, you will find few women singers participating in the Tambú genres.

"Tambú is a local tradition that needs to be preserved," poet and performance artist Gilbert Bacilio emphasizes (personal communication, October 30, 1995). A regular advocate for governmental recognition and support of Tambú and other Afro-Curaçaoan art forms, Bacilio helped establish Curaçao's annual Tula Festival, commemorating the ill-destined 1795 slave revolt. Festival highlights include performances by local Tambú bands because, according to Bacilio, "For us to remember the great freedom fighter Tula [one of the initiators of the revolt], we must use the voice of that history—Tambú." Increasingly, the act of representing and memorializing Africa has become the province of a growing guild of Curaçaoan professionals—anthropologists, musicians, visual artists, historians—who use Tambú as an attempt to regulate public memory.

"Tambú is a museum," says a young woman in response to the folkloric Tambú (Liesje, personal communication, December 28, 2001). From her perspective, the Tambú has emerged as a space of artifacts, presented to the audience as a sort of mnemonic device: a place where Curaçaoans can remember Africa and where the African ancestors can be symbolically remembered. To repeat her views, encountered in chapter 5, "Going to Tambú once or twice is fine. But who wants to go to the same museum, again and again, day after day, week after week?" These words raise certain questions regarding the role participation plays in maintaining a ritual's cultural and historical significance. Moreover, her words shed doubt on the tenacity of memory when it deals exclusively with the telling of historical facts, versus the interactive sharing in those facts.

"Tambú is a slave dance," says one Dutchman following the performance of a hotel-arranged Tambú; "a fight between slaves," another adds; "danced after a harvest, right?" a third gentleman asks. Among hotel-goers, perceptions of Tambú evolve out of isolated slivers of information, which they then use to base their own notions of Afro-Curaçaoan culture and history. Tourists often return home with impressions made and tastes formed as a result of these hotel "cultural shows," their perception of Tambú now representative of the African New World experience.

"Tambú is Christmas! When I hear Tambú I know that Christmas is coming!" the seven-year-old girl proudly confesses as her eyes widen, her voice growing more excited as she explains, "[Tambú is about] opening presents; a visit from *Sinter Klaus;* [and] lots of Christmas lights hanging on the trees" (Yomaida, personal communication, August 16, 2003). Her definition adds emphasis to the ongoing paradox—Tambú as ritual represents a quest for remembering; yet Tambú as Christmas music portrays complacency in forgetting. Commonality, if it exists, may lie only in the fact that both polar aspects of Tambú emerged in response to external forces.

To ask what Afro-Curaçaoans remember through Tambú generates a debate over who defines cultural memory, what counts as cultural memory, and, indeed, what cultural memory means. In studying Tambú, we develop an understanding of how cultural memory operates, and we gain insights into how ritual constructs can nurture a community's concept of "nation." Memory and history defy normal boundaries; they move freely between one realm and another, constantly shifting in terms of meaning and context. Memory fades, strengthens, or otherwise evolves with the inexorable passing of time. The past illumines modern cultural communities through the selective lenses of time, defining cultural communities selectively. Time and memory are inextricably interwoven, representing an ongoing dynamic from which our autobiographies—the stories we tell about our lives—are born. We cannot hope to understand memory's fragile power without examining what happens to memory as time passes, and considering how we translate the residues of experience that persist across time into tales of who we are.

◇ ◇ ◇ ◇ ◇

As the evening's first Tambú draws to a close, dancing temporarily ceases. *"Poné Bo Kla! Poné Bo Kla!"* the pregon intones the end of one ritual, the simultaneous beginning of another. "Get Ready! Get Ready!" Hands at our sides, we contemplate his words, which briefly hang in the air. The ensemble prepares for the next Tambú as the pregon shares local gossip, exposes the perceived misconduct of some dubious politician, reveals the extramarital affairs of this or that local individual. We silently review our own recent shortcomings, suddenly aware no one is immune from the pregon's discourse. The air of relief attending the beginning of the new Tambú reveals us not alone in that awareness! And with our lives free, at least for now, from critical Tambú revelation, our attention focuses on the next song.

Tonight's cultural celebration of the age-old Tambú tradition of dancing away *fuku* reflects both historical and political implications. A tent erected in an outdoor recreational area is festooned with strands of straw hung from the roof in emulation of the traditional *hòfi* setting. Here the old mixes with the new, reminds us of the extent to which both the Dutch authorities and the Curaçaoan blacks themselves have used Tambú as a vehicle through which to perceive the past and to control the present. Thus the evolution and development of the modern Tambú are displayed, the shaping of people's responses to it revealed.

And what of the politics of memory? Like the pages of a history book, *"Poné Bo Kla!"* bespeaks Curaçao's African past, recalls the myriad forms of Tambú. The evening progresses with one Tambú following another. We listen, we dance. We sing and clap our hands. The Tambú event is entertaining, and we appreciate the opportunity of reuniting with old friends; the chance to make new ones. After several hours, the Tambú singer steps forward announcing the evening's final Tambú. With the news, we quickly crowd the dance floor, determined to participate in the closing song. As it ultimately reaches an end, we enthusiastically applaud and shout. Some audience members raise their fists as a symbol of supportive recognition.

It is time to leave for the night, to slide back into the relative comfort of our lives, to leave the Tambú behind. The evening's experience now begins its own process of becoming a distant memory—one to be resurrected at a time of our own choosing, like a book placed back upon the shelf, there to await a future reading: *"Até aki, e historia di Tambú!"* "Here it is, the history of Tambú!"

GLOSSARY OF TERMS
REFERRING TO TAMBÚ

a capella   When a singer or group of singers perform without accompaniment, the style is called a capella.

afirmashon   Translated as "affirmation," the afirmashon refers to the vocal responses offered by the coro during the será section of the Tambú, used specifically to answer the pregon's calls.

agan di dos pida   Agan di dos pida is one of five basic types of herú (iron instruments) indigenous to Curaçao. Literally translated as "iron in two pieces," this particular instrument uses one tube, split down the side and open at each end, and one additional iron bar. Able to be played while standing up, the performer of agan di dos pida would often dance and move among participants during the Tambú performance.

agan di tres pida   Agan di tres pida is one of five basic types of herú (iron instruments) indigenous to Curaçao. Literally translated as "iron in three pieces," this particular instrument is the oldest of the herú types. It consists of two thick iron bars and one long iron tube. The tube, split down the side and open at each end, is held between the knees, its split side facing up. Played while seated, the tube is struck with an iron bar in each hand, producing tones and pitches according to where the tube is hit, and by which of the two bars.

Antillean waltz | The Antillean waltz denotes a music and dance genre from the Netherlands Antilles, often associated with Curaçao, which blends the European waltz form with local Spanish and African elements.

Arjuna | Javanese culture, a synthesis of Hindu, Buddhist, and Islamic influences, is celebrated in the shadow puppet theater of Wayang. One of the popular characters from Wayang is Arjuna, a Pandawa warrior, who exemplifies a refined and noble character. Arjuna was introduced to Tambú by Surinamese immigrating to Curaçao in the twentieth century.

Bandabou | Bandabou refers to that region comprising the westernmost tip of Curaçao.

Bandariba | Bandariba refers to that region comprising the easternmost tip of Curaçao.

bandera | Bandera refers to the small flags or bits of colored paper used in Bandera di Tambú, upon which were inscribed words and phrases to be used as themes for improvised Tambú songs.

Bandera di Tambú | Bandera di Tambú refers to a distinctive form of Tambú popular during New Year's. Translated as "Tambú of the Little Flags," this Tambú type involves small flags or bits of colored paper (called bandera) upon which were inscribed words and phrases to be used as themes for improvised Tambú songs. Bandera di Tambú were notorious for vulgarities and lies, gossip and ideas, that most preferred to write down anonymously rather than express aloud.

barí | Another name for the Tambú drum is barí, which literally translates as "barrel."

bonu-men | In the Winti religion, the priests are referred to as bonu-men. Many of the current religious leaders in Tambú are from Surinam, where they are recognized as powerful bonu-men.

brassa

Brassa refers to the hand clapping used during the será section of the Tambú. Brassa follows specific rules: one hand must be held outstretched, fingers and palm held upwards, while the other hand hits it smartly before springing backwards; this is then repeated in reverse, with the hands exchanging roles. This creates a specific rhythm, called the brassa rhythm.

Brua

Translated from Papiamento as "witch," *brua* is the term commonly used today to define the religious events surrounding Tambú.

Buddha

Buddha (literally "Awakened One" or "Enlightened One") is a title used in Buddhism for anyone who has discovered enlightenment. The Buddha is frequently represented in the form of statues. A personification of Buddha is requested during some Tambú rituals when fortune and good health are sought.

Byla di pelvis

Literally translated as "Dance of the Pelvis," it was one of several epithets popularly used by the Catholic Church in sermons and commentaries as a strategy for limiting Tambú participation.

Byla pa tira fuku afó

Byla pa tira fuku afó (translates as "dance to get rid of bad spirits") refers to a cleansing ritual prescribed by an obeah-man or -woman that involves dancing and sweating to Tambú as a way to counteract fuku. It is often organized as part of Manda Fuku Bai or Paranda di Tambú.

chapi

The chapi is one of five basic types of herú (iron instruments) indigenous to Curaçao. Literally the metal end of a common garden hoe, the chapi produces a loud, uniquely high-pitched tone when struck with an iron bar. The most commonly used herú in contemporary Tambú (both sacred and secular) is the chapi.

Condomblé

Condomblé is the name of the Afro-syncretized religion that emerged in Brazil among the slave communities. Although banned by the Catholic Church and government, Condomblé managed to thrive for over four centuries, becoming today a major, established religion with followers throughout Brazil.

Comback	Comback, a vernacular version of the English term "comeback," represents a popular party event on Curaçao, highlighting traditional Cuban music played by a disc jockey or performed by a live band.
coro	In Tambú, the chorus of singers, who usually participate in call and response with the pregon, is called the coro.
cotie	Cotie refers to the process by which sheep skin is made smooth and hairless through frequent soaks in a mixture of chalk and water.
creolization	The term *creole* derives from the Spanish *criadillo* (a diminutive form of the word *crido,* or "created one"). While originally the term *creole* denoted an individual of French or Spanish descent born in the Americas, it soon evolved to refer most commonly to New World blacks and people of color. By extension, creolization refers to the alloy process by which new African-based cultures emerged from the New World melting pot as autonomous entities.
cumbia	Cumbia is a dance music from Colombia comprising elements from the country's indigenous peoples, the Spanish, and the enslaved Africans, set in a ¼ rhythmic structure.
deklarashon introduktorio	Deklarashon introduktorio refers to the short, declamatory introduction in a Tambú song, generally sung by one solo singer. Its purpose is to announce the song's title or basic theme to the audience and surrounding musicians.
Eshu	In the Afro-syncretized religions, the deity considered the intermediary between the human and spiritual worlds is Eshu (also known as Legba, Ellegba, Ellegua, and Ellegbara). Eshu stands at the spiritual crossroads, giving (or denying) access to the spiritual world.

fuku	Fuku refers to the bad spirits that cause life's heaviest challenges. A specific Tambú was created to rid the bad spirits. Called Manda Fuku Bai, it drives away the fuku through singing, dancing, and the burning of incense.
gaita	The gaita is a musical style that originated in the Maracaibo region in Venezuela. Originally associated with Christmas, the gaita is presently played throughout the year.
Grupo Trinchera	Grupo Trinchera is a Tambú performance ensemble led by Rene Rosalia.
guajira	The guajira, a subgenre of the son, combines Spanish traditions with Hispanic melodies to create a new syncretized form that celebrates rural life and the Cuban countryside with romaticized nostalgia.
habrí	Tambú is in binary form. The first section is called habrí, which literally translates as "open." In this section, the pregon communicates the central storyline, with the audience (and coro) expected to stand in quiet reflection.
herú	Iron instruments are central to Tambú and, collectively, are known as herú. Although the rhythmic component is certainly pronounced in the role of the iron, the herú also serve to enhance the Tambú melody. They provide a polyrhythmic backdrop to the Tambú drum, their varied pitches creating cross-rhythmic harmonies.
hòfi	A hòfi is the name for the garden grounds of a former slave plantation home.
idiophone	The idiophone is one of four divisions of the Hornbostel-Sachs musical instrument classification system. An instrument that creates sound primarily by way of the instrument itself vibrating is classified as an idiophone.
kalbas den tobo	Kalbas den tobo, which translates as "calabash in a tub," is a drum indigenous to the Netherlands Antilles that makes use of a wooden wash tub filled about three-quarters full of water, with a large calabash half floating on

	top. With the tub serving as a resonator, the calabash is hit with two pieces of wood which have small pieces of cloth tied to their ends. Kalbas den tobo, while only an occasional drum substitute in Tambú, is central to Seú.
ka'i orgel	The ka'i orgel is a mechanical barrel organ first imported to Curaçao in the 1880s by the Dutch. The instrument uses a single crank to rotate a metal cylinder with precisely located pegs and pins to open and close valves corresponding to notes on the organ's keyboard.
kaseko	Kaseko is a musical genre from Surinam that fuses African, European, and U.S. American styles.
klabu-klabu	Klabu-klabu refers to a ritual cleansing bath prescribed by an obeah-man or -woman to ensure better fortune, often organized as part of Manda Fuku Bai or Paranda di Tambú.
kokomakaku	The kokomakaku was the stick fighting dance form that emerged on Curaçao, its name taken from the island shrub *coco maque* from whose trunks fighting sticks were traditionally constructed.
landhuis	The landhuis refers to the plantation house of slave proprietors. Manquerons were often quartered on the grounds of the landhuis estate.
Loango	Loango, also called Brama Kingdom, refers to a former African state in the basin of the Kouilou and Niari rivers (largely the southwestern region of the Republic of the New Congo). On Curaçao, the word "Loango" is translated as "African," and in modern usage is strictly an expression of insult, implying an affinity to things African. Considered an even more degrading insult of late is Preto Loango, which translates as "Black African."
lwa	Lwa (also known as loa) is the name used to define a deity from Haitian Vodou.
Manda Fuku Bai	Manda Fuku Bai was a traditional Tambú event performed for purposes of driving away bad spirits (called fuku). Although the event could be scheduled any time

during the year, the most popular occasion was during New Year's, when it was particularly hoped Tambú would chase away last year's fuku and initiate good fortune for the coming year.

manquerons   Literally translated from Papiamento as "unsaleable ones," *manquerons* was the term used to denote those Africans who arrived on Curaçao for purposes of slavery but, due largely to illness or old age, were marked unsaleable, and, therefore, remained on Curaçao, generally pressed into service as common laborers.

mariachi   Mariachi is a type of musical group originally from Mexico, comprising violins, trumpets, Spanish guitar, vihuela (a high-pitched, five-string guitar), and guitarrón (a small-scaled acoustic bass that is strummed). The music of the mariachi band is often referred to by the general term of "mariachi."

May Movement   The oil revenues at Shell skyrocketed during the 1960s, matched by a corresponding growth in new government positions of authority. When Shell filled these evolving positions again and again with Dutch-born civil servants, Curaçao's white and black population joined forces, marching in protest from the refinery to Fort Amsterdam to express their discontent on May 9, 1969. A riot ensued, now known as the May Movement. Although it resulted in only minor changes in the island's political system, its impact on Curaçaoan culture was significant and long-lasting.

merengue   The merengue is a music and dance form from the Dominican Republic that, promoted by Rafael Trujillo, president in the 1930s, assumed national status and is enjoyed today around the world. Its distinct instrumentation includes the tamboura, a two-sided drum played on the lap with palm and stick, and the güira, a sheet of serrated metal shaped into a cylinder and played with a stiff brush. In the Curaçaoan version of the Dominican merengue, the güira is replaced with the wiri.

Montamentu	The religion to which Tambú served as accompaniment was called Montamentu during the years of slavery. Montamentu purposely equated specific African deities with corresponding Catholic saints, while simultaneously paying homage to African and Amerindian ancestral spirits.
negotie slaven	Literally translated from Dutch as "slaves for trade," negotie slaven was the term used to denote the large number of Africans arriving on Curaçao and then sold into slavery elsewhere in the New World.
Netherlands Antilles	The Netherlands Antilles (Dutch: Nederlandse Antillen), previously known as the Netherlands West Indies, had comprised the windward islands of Aruba, Bonaire, and Curaçao (located in the eastern end of the Caribbean Sea, often referred to collectively as the ABC Islands) and the leeward islands of Saba, Sint Eustatius, and Sint Maarten (located in the north). In 1986 Aruba became an independent entity, and in 2010 the Netherlands Antilles was dissolved, resulting in Bonaire, Sint Eustatius, and Saba becoming "public bodies" of the Kingdom of the Netherlands, and Sint Maarten (which shares its island with Saint Martin, a French sovereign nation) and Curaçao becoming constituent countries within the Kingdom of the Netherlands.
New Holland	New Holland refers to an area of northeastern Brazil, including Recife and Pernambuco, which was ruled by the Dutch during the seventeenth century.
nobel barrels	Nobel barrels refer to those Tambú drums painted in the red, white, and blue colors of the Dutch flag. This practice emerged among Tambú participants as a possible way to thwart efforts by the government to destroy Tambú drums. With drums painted in this way, it was hoped authorities would refrain from damaging them.
Obeah-man or -woman	In the sacred Tambú, the spiritual head is known by the title of Obeah-man or -woman, a term borrowed from the English Caribbean.

Ogun	Ogun is generally considered the god of iron in the Afro-syncretized religions of the New World.
orisha	Orisha is the name used to define a deity from Santería.
Otrobanda	Otrobanda is considered one section of the city Willemstad. It was founded in 1707 (making it the newer section of the city) and translates from Papiamento as "The Other Side." Otrobanda and Punda are separated by a port channel, Sint Annabaai, and are connected by a pontoon bridge, the Queen Emma.
Papiamento	Papiamento is the local creole language indigenous to Curaçao that blends Portuguese, Dutch, Spanish, and a myriad of West African languages.
Paranda di Tambú	Paranda di Tambú refers to a distinctive form of Tambú that is distinguished for its tendency to move from place to place. Translated as "Tambú Parade," Paranda di Tambú became especially popular on New Year's Eve, involving participants marching from house to house, or from neighborhood to neighborhood, to the rhythms of Tambú.
parzee	*Parzee* (which translates as "party") was a term used to distinguish the secular Tambú type from the sacred.
Pincho y su Grupo	Pincho y su Grupo is a Tambú performance ensemble led by Pincho.
pisotea	Pisotea refers to the foot stomping used during the será section of the Tambú. Pisotea follows specific rules: one heel must be grounded in place, while the toes of the free foot stomp in time to the drum. This creates a specific rhythm, called the pisotea rhythm.
pregon	In Tambú, the lead singer is called pregon.
Punda	Punda is considered one section of the city of Willemstad. It was established in 1634, when the Dutch first captured the island from Spain. Translated from Papiamento as "The Point," Punda was originally called De Punt, the Dutch translation for "The Point." Punda and Otrobanda

are separated by a port channel, Sint Annabaai, and are connected by a pontoon bridge, the Queen Emma.

St. Miguel St. Miguel (St. Michael) is the Catholic Archangel, sought as a revered protector and guardian. In Tambú, St. Miguel is associated with the specific African deities Ellegba and Ogun.

salsa Salsa (literally translated as "hot sauce") emerged as a descriptive term to define popular Cuban-derived musical genres (like chachacha, rumba, and mambo). In the mid-1970s, the music was further developed by Cuban and Puerto Rican immigrants living in the New York City area.

Santería Santería is the name for the Afro-syncretized religion found on Cuba, the Dominican Republic, and Puerto Rico.

será Tambú is in binary form. The second section is called será, which literally translates as "closed." This section emphasizes participation, with the coro joining the pregon in call and response, and the audience responding in dance.

Seú Seú is a harvest ritual that emerged among the manquerons on Curaçao as a vehicle for ensuring successful food harvests. It is performed prior to planting and again at harvest time.

Shango Shango is generally considered the god of thunder in the Afro-syncretized religions of the New World.

Shon Shon was the term used by Afro-Curaçaoans during slavery to denote a slave proprietor. Today, the term *Shon* is used as a mark of respect, usually toward an elder within the community.

son The son is a five-note, bi-measure pattern emerging out of Cuba that comprises a "strong" measure containing three notes and a "weak" measure containing two, serving as the foundation for most rhythmic styles in contemporary salsa music.

Sounda di Tambú	Sounda di Tambú literally translates as "Play the Tambú" and refers to a distinctive form of Tambú that was performed for purposes of nourishing the soul of the Tambú drum. The event commenced when one or more participants called out the phrase, "Sounda di Tambú!" Two participants would then battle with kokomakaku sticks. When blood was drawn, the fighting stopped, and a measure of blood would be gathered and placed into a prepared hole in the dirt near the drum. The blood, it was believed, would ensure that the spirit of the drum remain healthy and strong.
Tambú	The term Tambú is used interchangeably to define the specific drum instrument (in which case the word is lowercased), the dance, the song, and the occasion itself.
Tambú di Kas	Tambú di Kas (literally translated as "Tambú for Houses") refers to a distinctive form of Tambú meant for indoor performances.
Tambú di Sanka	Tambú di Sanka literally translates as "Dance of the Behind." It was one of several epithets popularly used by the Catholic Church in sermons and commentaries as a strategy for limiting Tambú participation.
Tambú dóble	Tambú dóble (which literally translates as "double Tambú") refers to an event where two Tambú are going on simultaneously.
Tambú Season	Because many of the rigid ordinances against secular Tambú were temporarily lifted during the months of November, December, and January, thereby enabling more opportunities for Tambú performances, the allotted months have become known as Tambú Season.
tambúrero	Tambúrero refers to the player (traditionally male) of the Tambú drum.
trankamentu	Trankamentu refers to a confrontational game that evolved during slavery. Involving playful pushing and shoving between participants, the trankamentu, should participants get carried away, may escalate into a kokomakaku, the battle with sticks.

triangel   The triangel is one of five basic types of herú (iron instruments) indigenous to Curaçao. This particular instrument consists of an iron bar bent into a triangular shape. Held one-handed in a manner allowing optimum tone, the triangel was struck with a second iron bar.

trúk di palu   Trúk di palu (translates as "wooden pickup truck") refers to the transport by which some participants of the Paranda di Tambú would travel during the procession. The trúk di palu was often used when the Tambú parade would cover great distances.

trúk'i pan   Trúk'i pan (translates as "bread truck") is the name for the roadside snack truck, popularly located throughout the island. Serving sandwiches and local drinks, the trúk'i pan is generally open for business from around 9:00 PM to daybreak.

Tula   Tula is the name of the Curaçaoan-born slave who, with Louis Mercier, led the 1795 revolution, which involved about seventy manquerons from the Knip plantation (located along the island's southwestern coast).

tumba   The tumba is a Curaçaoan music genre whose pulse is dominated by the rhythmic juxtaposition of a triple meter over a duple. Deriving from slave origins, the tumba is not directly associated with any religious ritual, and as such remains free of the negative associations often affixed to Tambú.

Tumba Festival   Following the May Movement, the tumba was integrated (in 1971) into Curaçao's Karnaval, with musicians enthusiastically competing for the title of Tumba King or Tumba Queen, and passionately vying for composer of the Karnaval Tumba Road March. The scheduling of the Tumba Road March competition would occur four weeks prior to Lent, which, named the Tumba Festival, is a three-day competition beginning with preliminary contests, leading up to the finals held on the third day— which draws the largest audience.

Veve	Veve is the term used to define the symbolic designs drawn on the ground to invoke the arrival of a particular spiritual deity to a Tambú ceremony. It is a term borrowed from Haitian Vodou.
Vishnu	Vishnu is a form of God to whom Hindus pray. Recognized for his acute ability to preserve the world by incarnating himself in different forms at times of crisis, Vishnu was adopted into Tambú's pantheon of deities.
Vodou	Vodou is the name of the Afro-syncretized religion that emerged in Haiti among the slave communities. Other spellings for the religion include Voodoo and Voudoux.
Yama Áwaseru òf lòs Nubia	Yama Áwaseru òf lòs Nubia refers to a distinctive form of Tambú performed by a single drum soloist (with neither herú nor accompanying text vocalization) for purposes of bringing rain. The drummer utilizes stylistic effects meant to replicate the sounds of a thunderstorm—thunder, lightning, the sound of falling raindrops—as a way of encouraging the clouds to bring the needed rain.
yamada	The opening vocal call used to initiate the opening of the será section is called yamada. The term was also used in conjunction with secret Tambú gatherings, whose start would be announced by a single muted slap by the drummer—called yamada.
Willemstad	Willemstad is the capital of Curaçao and comprises two sections, Punda and Otrobanda.
Winti	Winti is the name of an Afro-syncretized religion distinct to Surinam. Although Winti remained separate from Catholicism during slave years and contains few ideological ties to Tambú, it has emerged as an important influence in the modern sacred Tambú.
wiri	The wiri is one of five basic types of herú (iron instruments) indigenous to Curaçao. Made from a serrated piece of iron over which a thin iron bar may be scraped to produce a raspy timbre, the wiri, while rare in Tambú, remains a common accompaniment to the Antillean waltz.

BIBLIOGRAPHY

Alden, Dauril, ed. (1973). *Colonial Roots of Modern Brazil.* Berkeley: University of California Press.

Allen, Rose Mary. (1989). "Ta Cuba Mi Ke Bai." *Afhankelijheid en Dominantie in de Antilles.* Amsterdam: Caraïbsche Werkgroep.

Améry, Jean. (1980). *At the Mind's Limits: Contemplations by a Survivor on Auschwitz and Its Realities.* Trans. Sidney Rosenfeld and Stella P. Rosenfeld. Bloomington: Indiana University Press.

Anderson, Benedict. (1983). *Imagined Communities: Reflections on the Origin and Spread of Nationalism.* London: Verso.

Ashcroft, Bill, Gareth Griffiths, and Helen Tiffin, eds. (1995). *The Post-Colonial Studies Reader.* London: Routledge.

Austin, John L. (1962). *How To Do Things With Words,* ed. J. O. Urmson and Marina Sbisà. Oxford: Oxford University Press.

Barlaeus, Casparus. (1647). *Rerum per Octennium in Brasilia.* Amsterdam: Blaeu.

Bell, Catherine. (1992). *Ritual Theory, Ritual Practice.* New York: Oxford University Press.

———. (1997). *Ritual, Perspectives and Dimensions.* New York: Oxford University Press.

Benjamin, Alan. (2002). *Jews of the Dutch Caribbean: Exploring Ethnic Identity on Curaçao.* New York: Routledge.

Bhabha, Homi. (1994). *The Location of Culture.* London: Routledge.

Boxer, Charles R. (1957). *The Dutch in Brazil, 1624–1654.* Oxford: Oxford University Press.

———. (1969). *The Portuguese Seaborne Empire, 1415–1825.* New York: Knopf.

Brada, Willibordus Menno. (1950). *Paters Jezueiten op Curaçao, 1700–1742.* Curaçao: Menkman.

Brenneker, Paul. (1961). *Curaçaoënsia.* Curaçao: Boekhandel Augustinus.

———. (1971). *Sambumbu: Volkskunde van Curaçao, Aruba en Bonaire.* Volume 3. Curaçao: Scherpenheuvel.

———. (1974). *Sambumbu: Volkskunde van* Curaçao, *Aruba en Bonaire.*
Volume 9. Curaçao: Scherpenheuvel.

———. (1975). *Sambumbu: Volkskunde van* Curaçao, *Aruba en Bonaire.*
Volume 10. Curaçao: Scherpenheuvel.

Bruner, Edward. (1986). "Ethnography as Narrative." In *The Anthropology
of Experience,* ed. Victor Turner and Edward Bruner. 139–156. Urbana:
University of Illinois Press.

Brusse, A. T. (1969). *Curaçao en Zijne Bewoners.* Amsterdam: S. Emmering.

Carby, Hazel. (1987). *Reconstructing Womanhood: The Emergence of the Afro-
American Woman Novelist.* New York: Oxford University Press.

Carter, Paul. (1987). *The Road to Botany Bay: An Essay in Spatial History.*
Boston: Faber & Faber.

Curtin, Philip D. (1969). *The Atlantic Slave Trade: A Census.* Madison:
University of Wisconsin Press.

Davis, Joseph. (2002). *Stories of Change: Narrative and Social Movements.*
Albany: SUNY Press.

De Jong, Nanette. (2003a). "An Anatomy of *Creolization:* Curaçao and the
Antillean Waltz." *Latin American Music Review* 24(2): 233–251.

———. (2003b). "Forgotten Histories and (Mis)Remembered Cultures: The
Comback Party of Curaçao." *British Journal of Ethnomusicology* 12(2):
135–151.

———. (2005). *Tambú, Seú, and the Ritual Process of Belonging.* Unpublished
paper presented at *Ondrozeck Lecture Series,* University of South Dakota,
Vermillion.

———. (2006). "'Joe'I Kórsou?' / 'Who Is the True Curaçaoan?' A Musical
Dialogue on Identity in Twentieth-century Curaçao." *Black Music Research
Journal* 26(2): 23–38.

———. (2007). "*Kokomakaku* and the (Re)Writing of History." *Afro-Hispanic
Review* 26(2): 87–101.

———. (2008). "Tambú: Commemorating the Past, Recasting the Present."
Transforming Anthropology 16(1): 32–41.

———. (2010). "The Tambú of Curaçao: Historical Projections and the Ritual
Map of Experience." *Black Music Research Journal* 20(2): 197–214.

Deren, Maya. (1972). *Divine Horsemen: The Voodoo Gods of Haiti.* New York:
Delta Publishing Company.

Desmangles, Leslie G. (1992). *The Faces of the Gods: Vodou and Roman
Catholicism in Haiti.* Chapel Hill: University of North Carolina Press.

Dominguez, Luis Arturo. (1988). *Vivencia de un Rito Luango en el Tambú.*
Caracas: Ediciones Co-Bo.

Edelman, Murray. (1995). *From Art to Politics: How Artistic Creations Shape
Political Conceptions.* Chicago: University of Chicago Press.

Edwards, Jay D. (1980). "The Evolution of Vernacular Architecture in the
Western Caribbean." In *Cultural Traditions and Caribbean Identity:*

The Question of Patrimony, ed. S. J. K. Wilkerson. 291–339. Gainesville: University of Florida, Center for Latin American Studies.

Emmer, Pieter. (1981). "The West India Company, 1621–1791: Dutch or Atlantic?" In *Companies and Trade,* ed. Leonard Blusse and Femme Gaastra. 71–95. Leiden: Leiden University Press.

Finkelstein, Joanne. (2000). "The Anomic World of the High Consumer: Fashion and Cultural Formation." In *Consumption in Asia: Lifestyles and Identities,* ed. Chua Beng-Huat. 225–240. London: Routledge.

Floyd, Samuel A. (1995). *The Power of Black Music: Interpreting Its History from Africa to the United States.* New York: Oxford University Press.

Giddens, Anthony. (1991). *Modernity and Self-Identity: Self and Society in the Late Modern Age.* Cambridge, U.K.: Polity Press.

Gilman, Sander. (1985). *Difference and Pathology: Stereotypes of Sexuality, Race, and Madness.* Ithaca, N.Y.: Cornell University Press.

Gomes Casseres, Charles. (1984). *One Hundred Years of Involvement: The Chamber and the Curaçao Economy, 1884–1984.* Curaçao: Kamer van Koophandel en Nijverheid te Curaçao [Curaçao Chamber of Commerce and Industry].

Goslinga, Cornelis Charles. (1956). *Emancipatie en Emancipator.* Assen, Netherlands: Van Gorcum.

———. (1971). *The Dutch in the Caribbean and on the Wild Coast, 1580–1680.* Gainesville: University Press of Florida.

———. (1977). "Curaçao as a Slave-Trading Center during the War of the Spanish Succession, 1702–1714." *West Indies Geschiedenis* 52: 1–50.

———. (1985). *The Dutch in the Caribbean and in the Guianas, 1680–1791.* Assen, Netherlands: Van Gorcum.

———. (1990). *The Dutch in the Caribbean and in Surinam, 1791–1942.* Assen, Netherlands: Van Gorcum.

———. (1993). *Een Zweem van Weemoed: Verhalen uit de Antilliannse Slaventijd.* Curaçao: Caribbean Publishing.

Hall, Stuart. (1989). "Cultural Identity and Cinematic Representations." *Framework* 36: 68–81.

———. (1996). "Diaspora Cultures: Roots and Routes." Keynote address, *Caribbean Culture Conference,* University of the West Indies.

———, ed. (1997). Introduction. *Cultural Representations and Signifying Practices.* 1–12. London: Open University Press.

Halbwachs, Maurice. (1980). *On Collective Memory.* Trans. Francis J. Ditter Jr. and Vida Yazdi Ditter. New York: Harper & Row.

Hamelberg, J. H. J. (1901). *De Nederlanders Op De West-Indische Eilanden.* Volume 1. Amsterdam: De Bussy.

Hartog, Johannes. (1956–1964). *Geschiedenis van de Nederlandse Antillean.* Aruba: Oranjestad.

———. (1961). *Curaçao van Kolonie tot Autonmie.* Aruba: De Wit.

Hartsinck, Jan Jacob. (1770). *Beschrijving van Guiana of de Wilde Kust, in Zuid-Amerika.* Amsterdam: S. Emmering.

Hill, Donald. (1998). "West African and Haitian Influences on the Ritual and Popular Music of Carriacou, Trinidad, and Cuba." *Black Music Research Journal* 18: 183–201.

Hoetink, Harry. (1958). *Het Patroon van de oude Curaçaose Samenleving.* Assen, Netherlands: Van Gorcum.

Honwana, Alcinda (1996). *Spiritual Agency and Self-Renewal in Southern Mozambique.* Ph.D. diss., University of London.

———. (1997). "Healing for Peace: Traditional Healers and Post-War Reconstruction in Southern Mozambique." *Peace and Conflict: Journal of Peace Psychology* 3: 293–305.

Iser, Wolfgang. (1972). "The Reading Process: A Phenomenological Approach." *New Literary History* 3: 279–299.

Janzen, John M., and Wyatt MacGaffey. (1974). *An Anthology of Kongo Religion: Primary Texts from Lower Zaire.* Lawrence: University of Kansas Press.

Juliana, Elis. (1976). *Guia Etnológiko. No. 1.* Curaçao: Drukkerij Scherpenheuvel.

———. (1983). *Orígen di Bale di Tambú na Korsou.* Curaçao: Kristóf.

———. (1987). "De Tamboe op Curaçao." *Bzzletin* 143: 59–65.

———. (1990). *Kiko ta pasa ku Tambú?* Paper. Curaçao: Centraal Historisch Archief.

Kammen, Michael. (1991). *Mystic Chords of Memory: The Transformation of Tradition in American Culture.* New York: Knopf.

Khan, Aisha. (2004). *Callaloo Nation: Metaphors of Race and Religious Identity among South Asians in Trinidad.* Durham, N.C.: Duke University Press.

Leitch, Thomas M. (1986). *What Stories Are: Narrative Theory and Interpretation.* University Park: Pennsylvania State University Press.

Lewis, John Lowell. (1992). *Ring of Liberation: Deceptive Discourse in Brazilian Capoeira.* Chicago: University of Chicago Press.

Lipsitz, George. (1990). *Time Passages: Collective Memory and American Popular Culture.* Minneapolis: University of Minnesota Press.

———. (1997). *Dangerous Crossroads: Postmodernism and the Poetics of Place.* London: Verso.

Liverpool, Hoolis "Chalkdust." (2001). *Rituals of Power and Rebellion: The Carnival Tradition in Trinidad and Tobago, 1763–1962.* Chicago: Research Associates School Times Publications.

Locke, David. (1996). "Africa/Ewe." In *Worlds of Music: An Introduction to the Music of the World's Peoples,* ed. Jeff Todd Titon. 67–106. New York: Schirmer Books.

Lowenthal, David. (1985). *The Past Is a Foreign Country.* Cambridge, U.K.: Cambridge University Press.

McAdams, Dan (1993). *The Stories We Live By: Personal Myths and the Making of the Self.* New York: Morrow.

McDaniel, Lorna. (1993). "Concept of Nation in the Big Drum Dance of Carriacou, Grenada." In *Repercussions of the 1492 Encounter,* ed. Carol Robertson. 395–410. Washington, D.C.: Smithsonian Press.

———. (1998). *The Big Drum Ritual of Carriacou: Praisesongs in Rememory of Flight.* Gainesville: University Press of Florida.

Mercier, Paul. (1954). "The Fon of Dahomey." In *African Worlds: Studies in the Cosmological Ideas and Social Values of African Peoples,* ed. Daryll Forde. 210–234. London: Oxford University Press.

Métraux, Alfred. (1972). *Voodoo in Haiti.* New York: Schocken Books.

Mintz, Sidney, and Richard Price. (1992). *The Birth of African-American Culture: An Anthropological Perspective.* Boston: Beacon Press.

Morgan, Philip D. (1997). "The Cultural Implications of the Atlantic Slave Trade: African Regional Origins, American Destinations and New World Developments." *Slavery and Abolition* 18(1): 122–145.

Neal, Arthur. (1988). *National Trauma and Collective Memory.* Armonk, N.Y.: M. E. Sharpe.

Nietzsche, Friedrich. (1957). *The Use and Abuse of History.* Trans. A. Collins. New York: Macmillan.

Ngũgĩ wa Thiong'o. (1997 [1981]). *Decolonising the Mind: The Politics of Language in African Literature.* Portsmouth, N.H.: Heinemann.

Nora, Pierre, ed. (1984–1992). *Les Lieux de mémoire* (seven volumes). Paris: Editions Gallimard.

———. (1996–1998). *Realms of Memory: Rethinking the French Past.* Trans. Arthur Goldhammer. New York: Columbia University Press.

Paula, Alejando F. (1978). *Problemen Rondom de Emigratie van Arbeiders uit de Kolonie Curaçao naar Cuba, 1917–1937.* Curaçao: Centraal Historisch Archief.

Pérez, Louis A. (1995) *Cuba: Between Reform and Revolution.* New York: Oxford University Press.

———. (1999). *On Becoming Cuban: Identity, Nationality, and Culture.* Chapel Hill: University of North Carolina Press.

Postma, Johannes. (1975). "The Origin of African Slaves: The Dutch Activities on the Guinea Coast." In *Race and Slavery in the Western Hemisphere,* ed. Stanley L. Engerman and Eugene D. Genovese. 33–49. Princeton, N.J.: Princeton University Press.

———. (1990a). *The Dutch in the Atlantic Slave Trade, 1600–1815.* Cambridge, U.K.: Cambridge University Press.

———. (1990b). *The Dutch Participation in African Slave Trade: Slaving on the Guinea Coast, 1675–1795.* New York: Cambridge University Press.

———. (2003). *The Atlantic Slave Trade.* London: Greenwood Press.

Pratt, Mary Louise. (1997). *Imperial Eyes: Travel Writing and Transculturation.* London: Routledge.

Price, Sally, and Richard Price. (1999). *Maroon Arts: Cultural Vitality in the African Diaspora*. Boston: Beacon Press.

Raboteau, Albert J. (1978). *Slave Religion: The Invisible Institution in the Antebellum South*. New York: Oxford University Press.

Rawley, James A. (1981). *The Transatlantic Slave Trade: A History*. New York: Norton.

Ricoeur, Paul. (1965). *History and Truth*. Trans. Charles A. Kelbley. Evanston, Ill.: Northwestern University Press.

Römer, René. (1977). *Un Pueblo na Kaminda: Een Sociologisch Historische Studie van de Curaçaose Samenleving*. Zutphen, Netherlands: Walburg Press [Ph.D. diss., University of Leiden].

———. (1981). *Samenlaven op een Caribisch Eiland: Een Sociologische Verkenning*. Curaçao: Van Dorp Eddine.

Rosaldo, Renato. (1988). "Ideology, Place, and People without Culture." *Cultural Anthropology* 3(1): 77–87.

Rosalia, Rene. (1992). *Mulina ta Mula Kaya Lo Bende (Yaba Yoatina II): Un Koleshon di Goreetika i Músika di Seú*. Curaçao (self-published).

———. (1994). *Tambú di Siglo 20*. Curaçao (self-published).

———. (1997). *Represhon di Kultura: E Lucha di Tambú*. Ph.D. diss., University of Amsterdam.

Rupert, Linda M. (1999). *Roots of our Future: A Commercial History of Curaçao*. Curaçao: Kamer van Koophandel en Nijverheid te Curaçao [Curaçao Chamber of Commerce and Industry].

Schacter, Daniel L. (1986). *Searching for Memory: The Brain, the Mind, and the Past*. New York: Basic Books.

Schwartz, Barry. (1991). "Social Change and Collective Memory: The Democratization of George Washington." *American Sociological Review* 56: 221–236.

Shelemay, Kay. (1980). "Historical Ethnomusicology: Reconstructing Falasha Liturgical History." *Ethnomusicology* 24(2): 233–258.

———. (1988). "Song and Remembrance." In *Let Jasmine Rain Down: Song and Remembrance among Syrian Jews*. Chicago: University of Chicago Press.

Small, Christopher. (1998). *Musicking: The Meanings of Performing and Listening*. Middletown, Conn.: Wesleyan.

Soest, Jaap van. (1977). "The World on an Island: The International Labour Force of Shell in Curaçao, 1915–1960." 1977 Conference Papers. Cave Hill, Barbados.

Tavares, Julio Cezar de Souza. (1984). *Dança de Guerra: Arquivo-Arma*. MA thesis, University of Brazil, Rio de Janeiro.

Thompson, Robert Farris. (1983). *Flash of the Spirit: African and Afro-American Art and Philosophy*. New York: Vintage Books.

Thornton, John K. (1988). "The Art of War in Angola." *Comparative Studies in*

Society and Culture 30: 362–365.

Trouillot, Michel-Rolph. (1995). *Silencing the Past: Power and the Production of History.* Boston: Beacon Press.

———. (2002). "Culture on the Edges: Caribbean Creolization in Historical Context." In *From the Margins: Historical Anthropology and its Futures,* ed. Keith Axel. 189–210. Durham, N.C.: Duke University Press.

Van Grol, G. J. (1941–1942). *De Grondpolitiek in het West-Indische Domein der Generaliteit. Een Historische Studie.* Netherlands: Gravenhage Algemeene Landsdrukkerij.

Van Meeteren, Nicolaas. (1947). *Volkskunde van Curaçao.* Curaçao: Drukkerij Scherpenheuvel.

Wagner, Roy. (1986). *Symbols That Stand for Themselves.* Chicago: University of Chicago Press.

Walker, Sheila S. (1972). *Ceremonial Spirit Possession in Africa and Afro-America: Forms, Meaning, and Functional Significance for Individuals and Social Groups.* Leiden, Netherlands: E. J. Brill.

White, Hayden. (1981). *Tropics of Discourse: Essays in Cultural Criticism.* Baltimore: Johns Hopkins University Press.

Wooding, Charles. (1981). *Evolving Culture: A Cross-Cultural Study of Suriname, West Africa, and the Caribbean.* Washington, D.C.: University Press of America.

Young, James Edward. (1993). *The Texture of Memory: Holocaust Memorials and Meaning.* New Haven, Conn.: Yale University Press.

INTERVIEWS

Because of the continued controversy surrounding Tambú, and because of possible social and religious retribution inflicted on those who have openly discussed the ritual with me, some names of people interviewed for this book have been changed (pseudonyms are indicated by an asterisk).

Alwin (Tambú ritual leader). Curaçao, December 29, 2001.*

Anita, Sherwin "Pincho" (Tambú singer and bandleader). Curaçao, December 29, 2001; January 2, 2002.

Bacilio, Gilbert (poet). Curaçao, October 30, 1995.

Etienne (Tambú ritual leader). Curaçao, August 10, 1998.*

Eugene (percussionist). Curaçao, August 5, 1997.*

Franklyn (*chapi* musician). Curaçao, August 10, 1997.*

Frederik (*snek truk* owner). Curaçao, December 30, 2001.*

Helena (mother and grandmother). Curaçao, August 6, 1998.*

Irceline (office worker). Curaçao, November 3, 1995.*

Layla (primary school teacher). Curaçao, January 2, 2002.*

Liesje (shop clerk). Curaçao, December 28, 2001; January 3, 2002.*

Lionel (drummer and percussionist). Curaçao, August 13, 1997; August 17, 2003.*

Maris (store manager). Curaçao, September 14, 1995.*

Martin (barber). Curaçao, January 2, 2002.*

Randall (percussionist). Curaçao, August 13, 2000.*

Reymound, Leonard "Magou" (percussionist). By telephone, November 20, 2000.

Rosalia, Rene (Director, Department of Arts and Culture; Tambú bandleader). Curaçao, September 29, 1995; August 13, 2000; December 30, 2001; January 5, 2002.

Rudsel (*chapi* musician). Curaçao, January 3, 2002.*

Rudy (disc jockey). Curaçao, November 4, 1995.*

Salsbach, Epifania "Fanny" (retired, police force; cruise ship tour guide). Curaçao, August 16, 1998.

Singh (disc jockey). Curaçao, January 5, 2002.*

Vernon (banker). Curaçao, August 8, 1997.*

Walter (jazz guitarist). Curaçao, August 10, 1997.*

Wendel (Tambú ritual leader). Curaçao, November 3, 1995.*

Willekes, John James (saxophonist and bandleader). Curaçao, October 3, 1995; August 13, 1997.

Wout, John (electric bass player and bandleader). Curaçao, August 10, 2003.

Yomaida (seven-year-old school girl). Curaçao, August 16, 2003.*

Yuchi (Tambú ritual leader). Curaçao, November 3, 1995.*

Zita (mother, grandmother, and great-grandmother). September 14, 1995.*

INDEX

Page numbers in italics refer to illustrations; page numbers in boldface refer to glossary entries.

a capella, **129**
afirmashon, **129**
African Diaspora, 120
Afro-Curaçaoans: affiliation with Afro-Caribbean religion, 77; Angolan population in Curaçao, 20; creolization and, 15–16; history of slavery and, 17–20; Othering of, 77–78; social status of, 117; Tambú as commemorative ritual for, 7; tourist perceptions of Africa and, 91–93; West African influence in, 24–25
agan (iron instruments), 24. *See also herú* (iron instruments)
agan di dos pida ("iron in two pieces"), 38, **129**
agan di tres pida ("iron in three pieces"), 37–38, **129**
allegory, 67
Alwin (Tambú ritual leader), 26, 83
Angola, 19–20, 22–23, 79
Anita, Sherwin. *See* Pincho (Sherwin Anita—Tambú singer and bandleader)
Antillean identity, 66
Antillean waltz, 3, 39, 90, 93, **130**
Arawaks: Arawak slavery in Curaçao, 7; influence on contemporary identity, 122; slave resistance of, 23; as Tambú spiritual ancestors, 75, 84;

treatment in *Montamentu*, 23; tree conservation practices, 31–32
Arjuna, 80–81, **130**
Aruba, 1n2
Ashcroft, Bill, 59
asiento slave trade, 24
Austin, John L., 68–69

Bacilio, Gilbert (poet), 126
Bandabou (Curaçao), 42–48, *46–47*, 65, 78–87, **130**
Bandariba (Curaçao), 65, **130**
bandera, **130**
Bandera di Tambú ("Tambú of the Little Flags"), 61–62, **130**
barí ("barrel" drum), 31–32, *39–40*, 56, 112, **130**. *See also tambú* (Tambú drum)
Bell, Catherine, 29
Benjamin, Alan, 122n1
Bhabha, Homi, 29
Black Box cable/internet, 74
Bonaire, 1n2
bonu-men, 74, **130**. *See also* Winti
Boxer, Charles R., 19
brassa (hand clapping), 41, *41*, 45, **131**
Brazil, 8, 19, 20, 23–24, 25, 120
Brenneker, Paul, 10, 20–21
British West Indies, 9
Browuer, Theodorus, 27

Brua ("witch"), 5, 29, 59, 65, **131**
Bruner, Edward, 5
Buddha, 74, **131**
Byla di pelvis ("dance of the pelvis"),
    64–65, **131**
Byla pa tira fuku afó, 61, **131**

Candomblé, 25
Cape Lahou, 18
capoeira (martial arts dance), 22
carnival, 66. *See also* tumba; Tumba
    Festival
Carpata, Bastiaan, 42
Carriacou, 118
Carter, Paul, 10, 69–70
Catholicism: appropriation of deities
    from, 28, 74, 80–85; folkloric
    Tambú and, 102–103; religious
    training of slaves, 8, 17, 27–28;
    Santería connection with, 28, 77;
    suppression of Tambú, 5, 7, 29, 45,
    47, 59, 120, 125–26; Tambú inte-
    gration of saints from, 4; Tambú
    satire directed toward, 63; threat
    of excommunication for Tambú,
    64–65
chapi (iron instrument): defined, 39,
    131; in the *deklarashon introduk-
    torio*, 45; description at Tambú
    ritual, 80; in folkloric performance,
    98; photos, *36–37;* at truk'i pan
    parties, 112. *See also herú* (iron
    instruments)
Chinese immigration, 74, 120
collective memory. *See* commemoration
Colombia, 7, 77
colonialism, 10–11, 15, 22. *See also*
    Dutch colonial government
Comback parties (Cuban-influenced
    parties), 3, 121, 123, **132**. *See also*
    party Tambú
commemoration: collective memory,
    6, 89–90, 119, 125–28; colonialism
    and, 10–11; commemorative ritu-

als, 124; construction of history
    and, 10; creolization and, 15; cul-
    tural crisis and, 119–20; emancipa-
    tion and, 28–29; folkloric perfor-
    mance and, 69, 125–27; history
    and, 49; memory and experience,
    5–6; remembered Africanness, 16,
    77, 80, 92–93, 117–20, 125; state-
    sponsored commemoration, 6;
    Tambú as commemorative ritual,
    7; Tambú Season cycle of, 103–105.
    See also forgetting; history
Condomblé, **131**
coro (Tambú chorus), 30, 40, **132**
cotie (sheepskin curing process), 32, *35*, **132**
creolization: defined, 15, **132**; blended
    New World deities and, 26–27, 74,
    118; Curaçao prison population
    and, 25; Curaçaoan identity and,
    120–23, 122n1; emancipation and,
    16; emergence of Tambú and, 4,
    20–22; *Montamentu* as symbol of,
    25–26, 29; West African shared
    identity, 24–25. *See also* identity
crossroads, 53
Cuba: *Combacks* and, 3, 121, 123;
    Cuban identity, 120–22; Curaçao
    prison population from, 25; as
    emigration destination, 4, 9, 9n5;
    influence on *Montamentu*, 26;
    Lucumi ritual, 118
cumbia, 123, **132**
Curaçao: Bandabao and Bandariba
    as favored Tambú areas, 65, 78;
    Chinese immigration, 74; colonial
    status of, 1, 119–20; contemporary
    cultural identity in, 120–23, 122n1;
    cultural diversity in, 2–3; descrip-
    tion of, 1–2; economic boom, 9;
    ethnic populations in, 8–10, 8n3,
    9nn4,5, 23; European colonization
    of, 7–8; Hanch'i Punda Street area
    (Willemstad), 60; map, *xviii;* na-
    tional discourse and, 89, 93, 103,

127; public memory in, 89–90; as slave trade center, 7–8, 49. *See also* economy
Curtin, Philip D., 19

Dahomey, 18, 24, 39
dancing: *capoeira* (martial arts dance), 22; cultural memory and, 69; description at Tambú ritual, 83; etiquette in, 42; in folkloric Paranda di Tambú, 99–101; *kokomakaku* dancing, 23; *pisotea* in, 41–42; suppression of, 29, 64–65; as Tambú New Year's tradition, 101–103; truk'i pan regulation and, 107, 111–16
danzón, 121
deklarashon introduktorio (Tambú introduction), 30, 40, 45, **132**
Desmangles, Leslie G., 75
Dominguez, Luis Arturo, 20
Dominican Republic, 9, 25–26, 77
Dutch colonial government: collective memory and, 6; economic interests of, 49; emancipation and, 29; oil boom of the 1960s and 1970s, 65–66; ordinances of cultural control, 52, 56, 58, 65; slave trade and, 8, 17, 27; treatment of *manquerons*, 17, 27, 28–29. *See also* Netherlands, Kingdom of the; suppression of Tambú

economy: *Bandera di Tambú* commercialism, 61–62; Curaçao economic environment, 117; Dutch colonial trade interests, 49; economic motive for slavery, 16; oil boom of the 1960s and 1970s, 65–66; post-emancipation plantation economy, 58; profitability of music performance, 105; Tambú Season commercialism, 104–105, 109–10, 113; tourism, 90–92

Ellegba, 26, 79. *See also Eshu*
Ellegua, 26. *See also Eshu*
emancipation: collective memory and, 28–29; creolization and, 16; post-emancipation plantation economy, 58; in Surinam, 81; as Tambú theme, 57–58. *See also* slavery
Eshu, 26, 50, **132**
Etienne (Tambú ritual leader), 26
Eugene (percussionist), 60
Ewe, 24

Finkelstein, Joanne, 67
Floyd, Samuel A., 48
folkloric performance: cultural memory and, 69, 125–27; folklorization process, 89, 103; May Movement and, 66, 89; performers' view of Tambú, 93–95; revival of New Year's Eve tradition, 101–103; Tambú parodies in, 88–89; tourist "cultural shows," 90–93, *91*, 127–28; Tumba Festival, 66
Fon, 24
forgetting, 5, 105, 124–25. *See also* commemoration
Franklyn (*chapi* musician), 36, 111
Frederik (*snek truk* owner), 107
fuku, 51, 101–103, **133**
funerals, 50–52, 56

gaita, 93, 123, **133**
gender, 25, 27–28, 42
gesturing tradition, 59
Ghana, 18
Giddens, Anthony, 67
Gilman, Sander, 78
global flows, 10, 73, 104–105
Goslinga, Cornelis Charles, 27
Grenada, 118
Grupo Trinchera, 35, *42–43*, *97–98*, 99, 109–11, **133**. *See also* Rosalia, Rene
guajira, 103, 121, **133**
guaracha, 121

habrí (Tambú "open" section): overview, 31, **133**; in *Bandera di Tambú,* 61; cultural plurality and structure of, 73; iron instruments in, 39; musical transcription of, *46;* standard rhythms for, *39;* structure of, 40–41, 73; summoning of *Eshu,* 50
Haiti, 25–26, 25n1, 28. *See also Veve* (spiritual drawings)
Halbwachs, Eric, 6
Hall, Stuart, 67, 69–70, 76
Hartog, Johannes, 62
Hartsinck, Jan Jacob, 18–19
Helena (mother and grandmother), 125–26
herú (iron instruments), 36–38, *39–40,* 53, 100, 102, **133**. See also *agan* (iron instruments); *agan di dos pida* ("iron in two pieces"); *agan di tres pida* ("iron in three pieces"); *chapi* (iron instrument); *triangel; wiri* (scraped metal instrument)
Hill, Donald, 118
history: *Montamentu* as dendrochronology, 16; public memory and, 10, 49, 89–90, 124, 128; Tambú as cultural history, 111. *See also* commemoration
hòfi (secret Tambú plantation grounds), 53–54, *54,* 99, **133**
hopps (drumhead retainer rings), 32, *34*

identity: African identity declining status, 78–79, 120; Antillean identity, 66; creolization and, 120–23, 122n1; Cuban identity, 120–21, 123; cultural identity in Curaçao, 120–23, 122n1; Dutch identity in Curaçao, 120–21; jazz and, 122–23; "Joe'i Kórsou?" ("Who Is the True Curaçaoan?"), 120–21; language and, 59, 66; remembered Africanness and, 16, 77, 80, 92–93, 117–20, 125; Tambú consumers and, 110; unified through Tambú singing

and dancing, 68–69; Venezuelan cultural identity in Curaçao, 123; West African shared identity, 24–25; youth identity, 4, 95, 113–14. *See also* creolization
idiophone, **133**. *See also herú* (iron instruments)
India, 120
Indonesia, 80–81. *See also* Arjuna
Irceline (office worker), 76
iron instruments. *See herú* (iron instruments)
Iser, Wolfgang, 68
Issoco, 95
Ivory Coast, 18

Jamaica, 25
jazz, 115, 122–23
Judaism, 8
Juliana, Elis: on *pisotea,* 41; research on Tambú, 10; on stick fighting, 20–21; on the suppression of Tambú, 29; on *Tambú* resolution of differences, 55–56; on trance rhythms, 50

Kafou Legba, 26. *See also Eshu*
ka'i orgel (mechanical barrel organ), 3, **134**. *See also wiri* (scraped metal instrument)
kalbas den tobo ("calabash in a tub"), 31, **133**
kalenda (Trinidad stick fighting), 20, 22
kaseko, **134**
Kennedy, John F., 74–75. *See also* Monroe, Marilyn
klabu-klabu, 61, **134**
Knip Plantation, 28, 42, 43
kokomakaku (stick fighting), 20–23, 42, 52, 56, **134**
Kromatine, 18

landhuis, **134**
Layla (primary school teacher), 99
Lebanon, 9

Legba, 26. *See also Eshu*
Liesje (shop clerk), 102
lieux de mémoire (places of memory), 119–20
Lionel (drummer and percussionist), 95–97
Lipsitz, George, 105, 122
Loango (expression of insult), 79, **134**
Loango (former African state), **134**
Locke, David, 69
Lwa (deity from Haitian Vodou), 26, **134**. *See also* Vodou

Manda Fuku Bai, 51, 102, **134–35**
manquerons ("unsaleable ones"): defined, 8, **135**; anti-white sentiment of, 52; black New World prisoners and, 25–26; colonial government treatment of, 27–28, 28–29, 49; food plots of, 51; post-revolt suppression of, 28–29; religious training and, 27–28; *Seú* (harvest ritual), 31, 90, **138**; social status of, 17; stick fighting competitions, 21. *See also negotie slaven* ("slaves for trade")
mariachi, **135**
Maris (store manager), 78
martial arts traditions, 22. See also *capoeira* (martial arts dance); *kalenda* (Trinidad stick fighting); *kokomakaku* (stick fighting); stick fighting
Martin (barber), 114
May Movement, 66, 89, **135**
McAdams, Dan, 124
McDaniel, Lorna, 18
media, 67, 74
memory. *See* commemoration
Mercier, Louis, 25n1, 28
Mercier, Paul, 24
merengue, 93, **135**
Mintz, Sidney, 4, 16, 25
Monroe, Marilyn, 75–76. *See also* Kennedy, John F.

Montamentu (religion associated with Tambú): defined, 3–4, **136**; ancestor worship in, 22–23, 75; appropriation of Catholicism in, 28, 74; Arawak influence in, 23; *asiento* era and, 24; black New World prisoners and, 25–27; *Brua* as term for, 65; christening of Tambú drums, 32; colonial government suppression of, 29; creolization as fundamental for, 25–26, 29; duplication of deities in, 26, 49–50, 74–75, 80–81, 83–85; lack of contemporary observance, 5; popular culture elements, 74–76; remembered Africanness as component of, 16, 77, 80, 92–93, 117–20, 125; slave-era status of, 17; treatment of Arawaks in, 23; West African influence in, 24–25
Morgan, Philip D., 15–16
musicking, 113

negotie slaven ("slaves for trade"), 8, 17, 27, 28, **136**
Netherlands, Kingdom of the: Caribbean colonies of, 1n2; Caribbean slavery and, 7–8, 19; colonial possessions of, 19; Curaçao relationship with, 1, 119–20; Dutch identity in Curaçao, 120–21. *See also* Dutch colonial government
Netherlands Antilles, 1, 1n2, **136**
New Holland, 8, 19–20, 23–24, **136**
newspaper function (of Tambú), 4, 30, 54–55, 57–58, 61–62
Ngũgĩ wa Thiong'o, 59, 77–78
Nietzsche, Friedrich, 5
nobel barrels, 56–57, **136**
Nora, Pierre, 119

Obeah-man/woman (spiritual leaders): defined, **136**; as creole component of *Montamentu*, 26; description at Tambú ritual, 79, 81–85; in folk-

loric Tambú, 101; role in posses-
sion, 50; in Tambú parades, 61
Ocalia, Aluisio, 60
oggán (Dahomean iron instrument), 39
Ogun, 79, **137**
oil industry, 9, 65–66, 73–74. *See also*
May Movement
orisha, 26, 118, **137**
Othering, 77–78
Otrobanda (Willemstad), 2, *96*, 102, **137**

Papiamento, 3, 45, 59, 66, **137**
Paranda di Tambú ("Tambú Parade"),
60–61, *96–100*, 98–101, **137**
party Tambú: *Combacks*, 3, **132**; Cuban
music at, 3; parzee (secular Tambú
"party"), 60, **137**; perception of
violence and, 113–16; police
chaperones at, 107; spiritual deities
at, 48; suppression of Tambú and,
59–60; truk'i pan and, 111–16.
See also Comback parties (Cuban-
influenced parties); *Tambú di Kas*
(house Tambú)
parzee (secular Tambú "party"), 60,
137. *See also Comback* parties
(Cuban-influenced parties); party
Tambú
Pincho (Sherwin Anita—Tambú singer
and bandleader): on *Bandera di
Tambú*, 62; as drum maker, 32;
photos, *108*; *Pincho y su Grupo*,
36, **137**; on songwriting, 107–109;
on Tambú Season, 105–106; on
tambureros, 33. *See also* "Poné Bo
Kla!" ("Get Ready")
Pincho y su Grupo, 36, 107–108, *108*,
110, 111, **137**. *See also* Pincho
(Sherwin Anita—Tambú singer
and bandleader)
pisotea (stomping/dancing), 41, *41*, 45,
50, 60, **137**
"Poné Bo Kla!" ("Get Ready"), xvi–
xvii, 12. *See also* Pincho (Sher-

win Anita—Tambú singer and
bandleader)
Portugal, 19–20, 23–24
possession: description at Tambú ritual,
83–84; engagement with appropriated deities, 75–76, 83–84; foot
stomp rhythms and, 50; in *kokomakaku*, 23; *Montamentu* rules of
possession, 49–50; in Paranda di
Tambú, 101; role of tambúrero in,
32–33; in secular Tambú, 60; in the
será section, 50
Pratt, Mary Louise, 68–69
pregon (lead singer), 30, 40, 63, 126–
27, **137**
Price, Richard, 4, 16, 25, 117
Price, Sally, 117
public memory, 89–90
Punda, **137**

Raboteau, Albert J., 75
radio, 67, 95, 104, 110
rain rituals, 51. See also *Yama Áwaseru
òf lòs Nubia*
Randall (percussionist), 60
Rawley, James A., 24
"Rebeldia na Bandabou" ("Rebellion at
Bandabou"), 42–48, *46–47*
religion: African religion as all-
embracing, 47–48; Angolan
ancestor worship, 22–23; black
New World prisoners and, 25–27;
Buddhism, 74, **131**; *Candomblé*, 25;
Judaism, 8; New World rituals, 118;
religious tolerance in Curaçao, 8;
religious training of slaves, 8, 17,
27–28; sacred and secular sharing,
47–48; Santería, 25–26, 28, 77, **138**.
See also Catholicism; *Montamentu*
(religion associated with Tambú);
religious Tambú; Vodou
religious Tambú: contemporary belief
in, 77, 86, 95, 96–97, 99–101; contemporary misunderstanding of,

76; cultural forgetting and, 5, 105, 124–25; functions of, 4; secrecy of, 3, 53–54, 76, 106; suppression of Tambú and, 59–60, 63–65. *See also* secular Tambú

resistance: Arawaks slave resistance, 23; disguised drums, 56; Haitian Revolution, 25n1, 28; *manqueron* anti-white sentiment, 52; May Movement, 66, **135**; *Montamentu/* Tambú as symbol of, 29; patriotic display as, 56–57; slave revolt of 1795, 25n1, 28. *See also* suppression of Tambú

resolution of differences function (of Tambú), 55–56

Reymound, Leonard "Magou" (percussionist), 62

rhythms: *barí* standard rhythms, *39–40; brassa* standard rhythm, *41; herú* standard rhythms, *39–40; kokomakaku* drum rhythm, 21; *pisotea* standard rhythm, *41;* in sacred and secular contexts, 47–48

Riguad (Tula), 28

Riguad, Benoit Joseph, 28

Romania, 9

Rosaldo, Renato, 10

Rosalia, Rene: on folkloric performance, 92; on funerals, 51; as *Grupo Trinchera* director, 35, 42–43; on language suppression, 59; on the origin of the *chapi,* 39; on *pisotea,* 41; research on Tambú, 10; on stick fighting, 21; at Tambú ritual (in Bandabou), 78–86; Tambú Season and, *96,* 97–98, 106; on Tambú suppression, 56–57, 64

Rouville, Governor, 63–64

Rudsel (chapi musician), 111

Rudy (disc jockey), 106

Saba, 1n2

St. Miguel, 79–85, *80–81,* **138**

salsa, 103, 122, **138**

Salsbach, Epifania "Fanny" (retired, police force; cruise ship tour guide), 101

sanga (war dances), 20

Sanger pa Tambú ("Blood of the Tambú"), 51–52

Santería, 25–26, 28, 77, **138**

satire, 22, 63–64

Schacter, Daniel L., 124

secular Tambú, 59–60, 63–65, **137.** *See also Comback* parties (Cuban-influenced parties); folkloric performance; *parzee* (secular Tambú "party"); religious Tambú; *Tambú di Kas* (house Tambú)

Sephardic Jewish immigration, 8

será (Tambú "closed" section): overview, 31, **138;** in *Bandera di Tambú,* 61; *brassa* and *pisotea* in, 45; cultural plurality and structure of, 73; group participation in, 69; iron instruments in, 39; musical transcription of, 47; standard rhythms for, *40;* structure of, 40–41, 73

Seú (manqueron harvest ritual), 31, 90, **138**

Seú (water drum), 91–92, *91*

Shango, 26, **138**

Shelemay, Kay, 49

Shell Oil, 9, 65–66, 73–74

Shon (as slave proprietor), 55–56, **138**

Singh (disc jockey), 67

singing: in *Bandera di Tambú,* 61, 63; call-and-response pattern, 60, 61; communal consciousness and, 69; description at Tambú ritual, 100–101, 102, 112–13; interactive interpretation and, 68–69; *kokomakaku* singing, 21–23; *pregon* (lead singer), 30, 40, 63, **137;** satire in, 63–64; women's diminished involvement in, 109, 126. See also *coro* (Tambú chorus); *pregon* (lead singer)

Sint Eustatius, 1n2
Sint Maarten, 1n2
slavery: abolishment, 8–9; Arawak
    slavery, 7, 23; *asiento* slave trade,
    24; Curaçao incarceration facilities,
    25; Curaçao slave trading center,
    8, 17, 20; economic motive for, 16;
    emergence of Tambú and, 4–5,
    20–22; history of Curaçao slavery,
    17–20; *manqueron* social status,
    17; Paranda di Tambú role in, 98;
    resistance movements, 23; ship log
    records of, 18; slave revolt of 1795,
    25n1, 28; stick fighting competi-
    tions, 21. *See also* emancipation;
    manquerons ("unsaleable ones");
    negotie slaven ("slaves for trade")
Small, Christopher, 113
son, 103, 121, 123, **138**
Sounda di Tambú, **139**
Spain, 7, 19, 23
spontaneity, 65, 106
standplaats (authorized languages),
    58–59
stick fighting, 20–21. See also *capoeira*
    (martial arts dance); *kalenda*
    (Trinidad stick fighting); *koko-*
    makaku (stick fighting); martial
    arts traditions
sugar industry, 9, 9n4, 19–20
suppression of Tambú: class stigma and,
    77–78, 86–87; cultural memory
    and, 124–25; emergence of secu-
    lar Tambú and, 59–60, 63–65;
    folkloric performance and, 66–67,
    89–90, 95; Othering of Afro-
    Curaçaoans, 77–78, 86–87; pub-
    lic misunderstanding and, 76;
    religious suppression of Tambú,
    5, 7, 29, 45, 47, 59, 120, 125–26;
    research on, 10; restrictions on
    dancing, 29, 64–65, 107; secrecy
    as consequence, 3, 53–54, 76, 106;
    Tambú Season restrictions, 5, 104,

106, 116; truk'i pan regulation,
    107, 111–16. *See also* Dutch colo-
    nial government; resistance
suppression of Tambú, particular
    ordinances: "rules against bad
    behavior" (1740), 52; prohibition
    of meetings (1741), 52; ban on
    Tambú singing (1750), 56; *koko-*
    makaku stick prohibition (1766),
    56; prohibition of threats to "over-
    all tranquility" (1780), 56; authori-
    zation of physical violence (1872),
    58; official language designation
    (1884), 58–59; permit requirement
    introduced (1935), 65
Surinam (Dutch Guiana), 9, 74, 80–81
Syria, 9

Tambú: defined, **139**; association with
    Africa, 16, 77, 80; emergence of,
    4, 20–22; as oral newspaper, 4, 30,
    54–55; research on, 10; resolution
    of differences function, 55–56;
    Tambú bands, 35–36, *37*. See also
    habrí (Tambú "open" section);
    Montamentu (religion associated
    with Tambú); religious Tambú;
    secular Tambú; *será* (Tambú
    "closed" section)
tambú (Tambú drum): overview, 31–32;
    construction of, 32; disguised
    drums, 56; open vs. closed palm,
    53; photos, *38;* playing technique,
    32–37; spirit housed in, 32
Tambú di Kas (house Tambú), 53–54,
    60, **139**. *See also* party Tambú
Tambú di lamentu ("Tambú of grief"), 65
Tambú di sanka ("Tambú of the be-
    hind"), 65, **139**
Tambú dóbel, 60, **139**
Tambú parades ("Paranda di Tambú"),
    60–61, *96–97*, **137**
Tambú parties. *See Comback* parties
    (Cuban-influenced parties); party

Tambú; parzee (secular Tambú "party"); secular Tambú Tambú ritual. *See* religious Tambú
Tambú Season: defined, **139**; association with Christmas, 105–106, 127; folkloric performance and, 66–67, *96*, 97–98; ritual origin of, 4; state restrictions and, 5, 104; Tambú bands and, 67, 105, 107–108; truk'i pan venues, 107; violence associated with, 113–16
Tambú structure: overview, 30–31; binary form, 21, 23, 31, 45, 48, 50, 59–60, 73, 118; interactive interpretation and, 68–69; *kokomakaku* and, 23; open door Tambú policy, 73; "Poné Bo Kla!" ("Get Ready"), 11–12; *pregon* role in, 40–41; at secular parties, 59–60; spiritual world access and, 50, 73, 118. See also *habrí* (Tambú "open" section); *será* (Tambú "closed" section)
tambúrero (Tambú drummer), 32–33, *38*, **139**
Thompson, Robert Farris, 27
Thornton, John K., 20
tourism, 90–92
trance. *See* possession
trankamentu (male competition in dancing), 42, 56, **139**
triangel, 38, **140**
Trinidad, 20, 22, 25, 55–56, 118
Trouillot, Michel-Rolph, 4, 16
trúk di palu, 61, **140**
truk'i pan, 107, 111–16, **140**
Tula, 28, 42–43, **140**
tumba, 66, 93, **140**
Tumba Festival, 66, **140**

van Grol, G. J., 23
Van Meeteren, Nicolaas, 54
Venezuela: Arawaks' relocation to, 8n3, 23, 84; as Curaçao emigrant destination, 23; as Curaçao exile destination, 23; discovery of gold in, 7; as Montamentu "promised land," 23, 51–52; religious training of slaves and, 8, 27–28; as source of Caribbean oil workers, 9; Venezuelan cultural identity in Curaçao, 123
verbal dueling, 55–56
Vernon (banker), 77
Veve (spiritual drawings), 26, 82, **141**. See also Vodou
Vishnu, 74, **141**
Vodou, 25–26, 28, 77, 118, **141**

Wagner, Roy, 67
Walker, Sheila S., 75
Walter (jazz guitarist), 101
Wendel (Tambú ritual leader), 26
West Indische Compaigne (WIC), 8, 17, 19–20, 24, 25, 27
White, Hayden, 67
Willekes, John James (saxophonist and bandleader), 97, 106, 125
Willemstad (Curaçao), 2, 93, 101–103, **141**
Winti, 74, **141**. See also bonu-men
wiri (scraped metal instrument), 3, 38–39, 88, **141**. See also Antillean waltz; *herú* (iron instruments)
Wout, John (electric bass player and bandleader), 106

Yama Áwaseru òf lòs Nubia, 51, *94*, 95–97, **141**. See also rain rituals
yamada (muted drum technique), 53, **141**
yamada (vocal call), 40, **141**
Yomaida (seven-year-old school girl), 105, 127
Yoruba, 24, 118
Young, James Edward, 6
Yuchi (Tambú ritual leader), 26, 50

Zita (mother, grandmother, and great-grandmother), 76–78

NANETTE DE JONG

is senior lecturer at the International Centre for Music Studies, Newcastle University. Her research examines the identities forged by African diasporic groups, emphasizing the ways in which these identities find expression in music. She has published on avant-garde jazz and Caribbean music in such journals as *Latin American Music Review, Afro-Hispanic Review, Transforming Anthropology, Jazzforschung/Jazz Research,* and *Black Music Research Journal,* and more recently has expanded her research to include the transatlantic journey of Afro-Caribbean and jazz rhythms returning to Africa through globalization. De Jong is also an accomplished classical and salsa flautist, serving as substitute flute with the Chicago Symphony Orchestra, and performing with such salsa greats as Johnny Pacheco and Celia Cruz.